With the Irregulars in the Transvaal and Zululand

With the Irregulars in the Transvaal and Zululand

The Experiences of an Officer of "Baker's Horse" in the Kaffir and Zulu Wars 1878-79

W. H. Tomasson

LEONAUR

With the Irregulars in the Transvaal and Zululand
The Experiences of an Officer of "Baker's Horse"
in the Kaffir and Zulu Wars 1878-79
by W. H. Tomasson

First published under the title
With the Irregulars in the Transvaal and Zululand

Leonaur is an imprint of Oakpast Ltd

Copyright in this form © 2012 Oakpast Ltd

ISBN: 978-0-85706-797-5 (hardcover)
ISBN: 978-0-85706-798-2 (softcover)

http://www.leonaur.com

Publisher's Notes

Contents

DEDICATED TO COLONEL REDVERS BULLER,
V.C., C.B., C.M.G., A.D.C.,
AND THE OFFICERS AND MEN
OF THE IRREGULAR HORSE
OF THE FLYING COLUMN,

Preface

Seeing how much even Regular Regiments prize the record of the services of their regiments, surely an Irregular Regiment should value such annals even more. In the one case, every gallant deed is handed down from generation to generation of officers and men; in the other, the regiment is disbanded, and its members scattered to the four winds of heaven. On these grounds I trust that this volume, which contains a few sketches of the deeds of the Irregular Cavalry of the Flying Column, may prove acceptable to some of its whilom members. They will, I hope, look indulgently over the mistakes in facts and style, of which, I am painfully conscious, there are many; I hope critics will do likewise, and remember that the hand that wrote would rather handle sword than pen.

Most Irregulars will not fail to discover Captain Watt Whalley's hand in not a few of these pages. To the public I confess the great assistance I have received from that officer; here is a receipt for them to discover his hand from the author's: all the sense is his, the nonsense mine. What little entertainment the reader derives from these pages they will owe him, as the author does the smatter of practical soldiering he possesses.

As my colonel and commandant used to say, finishing up a wigging to his officers, "as for the adjutant—the less said of him the better." Critics, say worse of his writing, I defy you to.

W. H. Tomasson

CHAPTER 1

Buller's Command

In the present state of South African affairs the following chapters, the notes of a march across North Basutoland and the Transvaal may be of interest. They are from the journal of an officer of one of the best-known Irregular Regiments.

On the 7th of July, 1878, the regiment left its headquarters near King William's Town and marched north. The Kei River was crossed on the 9th, and Fingoland entered. The Fingoes are the most loyal race of South Africa; we have redeemed these people from a life of abject slavery, and in return they are grateful. Gratitude is scarce in South Africa; the fact is therefore worth mentioning. Previously to our taking them in hand, they were veritable hewers of wood and drawers of water to their fiercer neighbours. They fought fairly under various leaders—Lonsdale, Pattel, and others during the Ghaika and Galeka wars of 1877. They submitted to be disarmed in 1880, but have had their arms restored, and are now fighting with us against the Tambookies, Basutos, and Tembus.

After Fingoland came the Tambookie Reserve. The Tambookies, a fairly warlike race, are now in arms against the Cape Government. The Bashee River was next reached; this stream formed the limit to the warlike operations of 1877-78 against Kreli. Here we enter Bomvanaland, inhabited by a race remarkable for pusillanimity. Most *kaffirs* will make a fight for their cattle, leaving his other belongings, such as wife, children, and huts to their own devices. However, we were told that these Bomvanas cannot be provoked to hostilities even by this grievous injury.

I regret I have never heard the course the Colonial Government adopted with respect to the country lying between the Butterworth and Bashe Rivers; neither have I learnt the fate of Kreli the chief of the country. He and his people fought right well for their independence, and fought honourably. He was supposed to be averse to war, but was overruled by his young men. Finding he could not avert bloodshed, he warned all European residents to quit his territory. In some instances he even supplied an escort for protection of life and property. In his case we hear nothing of those hideous atrocities that were committed by the Christian, and other adherents of Sandili, the Gaika chief in British Kaffraria.

Sandili, however, had the good fortune to fall in fight. Kreli is probably a wanderer from his beautiful country. And it is a glorious territory, with rich and fertile soil, noble forests, and abundance of water. It would be an admirable home for settlers. The only drawback discoverable during the weeks I patrolled the territory were the ticks. These attacked both man and beast in the immediate neighbourhood of the sea coast. The Colonial Governments have, however, always set their faces against emigration, no importation of small settlers having taken place since 1858. Then General von Stittenheim established his German legionaries in Kaffraria. These men were the relics of the German Legion raised for service in the Crimea. They started with absolutely nothing beyond a small grant of land, and a daily ration of food. Now the survivors and second generation are in very comfortable circumstances.

July 19. Rose at 3 a.m., packed waggons by moonlight. A severe frost, as indeed there was wherever we went, till arrival at Lydenberg, and afterwards in Zululand. Reach the settlement and river of Umtata at noon. Here is a bishop of the Church of England, a cathedral of corrugated iron, and some 30 or 40 houses scattered here and there, as though shaken out of a pepper box. On the west bank of the river a British magistrate seems to have some authority, he has been since murdered we believe. The owners of property on the other side have to deal with a Pondo chief Umkalese who levies taxes as he thinks proper. By sending a cow's tail to the settler he compels his (the trader's) attendance at his big *kraal*. One house, supposed to have been a hotel, is on the Pondo side, but does, or did no traffic in liquors on account of the heavy license demanded by this astute barbarian. What an example for the Middlesex magistrates. We left this spot after a day's halt, and saw thenceforward but few houses till arrival at Griqualand. The telegraph was opened between Natal and the Cape a few months previously. There is a European operative resident at the different stations few and far between.

July 22. Reach the Tina River, a noble affluent of the St. John's River. A day's halt, and much bathing and washing. All along this river, war is now, (1881), raging fiercely. The troops are under the command of Lieut.-Col. Baker, whose name figures frequently hereafter in this book

July 22. Camp on banks of the Umzimvubu or St. John's River proper. The scenery here is very grand, and the hill leading from the drift towards the eastward a feature to be remembered.

July 27. After crossing other large streams the 90th Light Infantry under Col. Wood was overtaken by us at a place 5 or 6 miles from Kokstad, on the borderland of Griqualand West.

July 28. The column thus united, marched, or rather scrambled into Kokstad. The hill up which the waggon had to be dragged was a real caution, and made us begin to understand the difficulty Colonel Wood had in getting transport riders to accompany his columns. His train was composed chiefly of ox-waggons, with owners or conductors of the nondescript Dutch-English breed, peculiar to the business of carrying in South Africa. It appears that these men were compelled to bring on their waggons so far from their houses in the Cape Colony, and to traverse this wild and almost unknown country. Their outcry against the Colonel as the waggons stuck was rich in oaths, both English and Dutch. However, by dint of unloading and reloading, and drag ropes hauled on by the troops, the thing was compassed somehow, and we found ourselves in Kokstad by 4 p.m. We had calculated on a good night's rest after this manual labour, but had to turn out the regiment during the night to put out a grass fire some three or four miles off.

Kokstad is so called after Adam Kok, who bought his Griquas here from Griqualand West (now the Diamond Fields). Here we remained three weeks, which were not unprofitably spent in drilling our men, many of whom had joined but a few days before leaving King William's Town. Kokstad has streets, and a magistrate, one or two churches and hotels. It is miserably cold in the winter at least. There was a sort of rebellion here which was easily suppressed, the only loss of life arising from the explosion of a powder magazine, by which I think several Europeans, amongst them some ladies, were killed or seriously injured. The place was garrisoned as we marched in by a company of the 3rd Buffs, and a detachment of Cape Mounted Rifles. The natives here are clothed in the European fashion. Adam Kok appears to have been a chief of great intelligence and capacity. A good ruler, and a friend to the English, his death was a loss to all parties.

During our stay at Kokstad, Captain Barton of the Coldstream Guards, attached to the regiment, went with some of the authorities to seek an interview with the Pondo chief. This journey had no result. The natives allowed the small party to come within sight; but declined to hold any intercourse, although they were in great numbers. These Pondos were evidently anxious not to give any cause of complaint, and wisely avoided arty discussion with the Cape authorities. Although they were guiltless of any act that could possibly be construed into a breach of the peace, they were prepared to pay over a large number of cattle to the authorities to be left in peace.

An English lady, by name Mrs. Jenkins, since dead, lived in their midst, doing good according to her lights. She appeared to exercise great influence over the chief Umiquikela and his councillors. She had one European companion of her own sex, who elected to share this isolated life with the old lady.

What the Cape Government wished to extract from these Pondos we could not hear. It appears, however, Mr. Sprigg, the Cape Premier, took advantage of this overland movement of troops to Natal— even if the march were not undertaken at his solicitation—to, pick a quarrel with these Pondos. These people were 200 miles from the Cape frontier, and were in no way concerned or interested in Colonial matters. They only wished to be allowed to manage their own affairs in their own way, which is mild and inoffensive enough. We have since wondered how Sir Bartle Frere and Lord Chelmsford allowed themselves to be made, in some measure, the tool of the astute Cape lawyer.

However, at the present moment, Jan., 1881, Mr. Sprigg seems to have succeeded in his policy of aggression, and to have raised a tolerably compact resistance to his scheme of Colonial supremacy. These schemes were successful enough in 1878 when the Colonial levies having failed to do anything, the Imperial troops came forward, and put an end to the conflict. It remains to be seen what the Colonists unassisted will accomplish. They, however, are largely supported by a staff of British regular officers. It is devoutedly to be hoped that they will be left to get out of their self-made difficulties as they best can, and that they will be disabused of the idea that the British taxpayer is to find the sinews of war, and the British army to bleed, while they reap the advantages of the expenditure.

On this occasion, Aug., 1878, Mr. Sprigg was unsuccessful in his attempts on the Pondos, and after three weeks' delay—which we afterwards found to be an irreparable loss—we were suffered to proceed on our road. We quitted Kokstad on August 19. Since then the Pondos were left in peace, unharrassed, while English troops were engaged fiercely in Zululand. After the close of the Zulu war a desperate attempt was made to stir them up. They could not, however, be induced to fight. Now, when the Cape Government's feeble hands are more than full with Basuto, Tambookies, Tembu, Pondomise and other wars, the Pondos are restive, and they are cowardly enough to pander to them, and by truckling hope to keep them quiet. It is to be hoped that the Colonial Office at home will take up their cause and look after them. They are much sinned against, and very little have sinned. Poor fellows, let once the other wars be over and their turn comes next, and they know it.

Therefore let us hope our own temperate Colonial Office will step in, and firmly and judiciously treat these good people. On the evening of the day we left Kokstad we crossed into Alfred County, Natal. The road cut through a northernly projection of that colony for a couple of miles. We had, at a house rejoicing under the name of Beast Kraal, a conversation with a huge Yorkshireman and his handsome wife. They had been attacked by the rebel Griquas who quitted the house without fortunately taking life. By way of committing extra damage they had thrown all the molasses they could find about the floor, and plucking the fowls they had killed, stuck the feathers into the treacle.

August 20. Reach civilisation, or rather partial civilisation, and cross the Umzimkulu into Natal. At the ferry is a telegraph-office, shops, and actually a billiard table. After this day we began to see houses, enclosures, and plantations of gum and fruit trees. There is also a good road, that portion descending the beautiful valley of the Umkomazi being really a work of science and labour judiciously combined.

August 24. Reach Pietermaritzburg, being played in by the infantry band. Tents are pitched just below Fort Napier. Thus ended a march which proves with what rapidity a well calculated movement can be effected, in an almost unknown country, nearly entirely destitute of roads and supplies. Leaving King William's Town on 7th July, Kokstad was reached on 28th. Total 22 days, of which 5 were halts. From Kokstad to Pietermaritzburg were 5 days. Total 22 days of march to go over 410 miles, or thereabouts, of as difficult a country, as in several years

15

of very varied service we had the good fortune to see. Our transport consisted of 8 ox waggons, carrying about 2200 lbs. each. Major, now Colonel Redvers Buller in command, proved to the satisfaction of all ranks, that he was as well qualified to organise, as to carry out.

From that time he was looked up to by all under his command, as a man who foresaw everything, and never erred in his calculations. At Pietermaritzburg, a few recruits were picked up, and a few good-for-nothings discharged. And on 29th August, 1878, the regiment set forth for the Transvaal Lady-Smith, 100 miles, was reached in four days. A day's halt, and three days more brought us to Newcastle, 180 miles from Pietermaritzburg. All this road was very fair being the main highway of the Colony. It had excellent bridges and but few very severe hills, such as present themselves on the more deserted eastern road by Greytown. The condition of the roads at this time was very different to what they were a year later, when the traffic of the store waggons bound for Zululand had completely destroyed them.

At Greytown another day's halt took place, and we took stock of the last English town we were likely to see for some time. Here we met, at a billiard table with some brother officers, the first Trans-vaal Boers we had seen. These people are not backward in opening conversation, and accordingly began to question us. They asked our purpose in marching, as to our domestic affairs, and fears, and hopes generally.

They were pleased to express approval of our going to fight Se-cocoeni. This was the Basuto chief who had given their ex-President Burgers so much thread to twist. They then, having satisfied their ample capacity for news, suffered us to dine in peace. We enjoyed the hospitality of the innkeeper, Mr. Hitchcock, afterwards killed at Isandhlwana.

It may here be not out of place to insert the colonial opinion of Dutchmen. A Boer is described as simple in some things, very few however, as a child, as acute in the majority as a Bristol Quaker, he is supposed to be endowed with the appetite of an ostrich, and the freedom from nicety of a vulture. To the weak, he is insolent, brutal and overbearing, to the strong he is either cringing, or takes refuge in stupidity, and a stolid sullenness. Morals he has none, and the crime of incest is rife, especially in the northern Transvaal. The women are without the natural delicacy of their sex, the men have no chivalry.

CHAPTER 2

The High Veldt

On the 8th September, while halting for breakfast at a farm-house owned by an Englishman, who supplied bundles of forage (oat hay) we found that we were in the Transvaal. The boundary line was marked by an inconsiderable brook. The next afternoon we reached the little hamlet of Amersfort. There is here a large shop, and a Dutch Church, served by the minister of Standerton. That day we began to understand the meaning of Hooge Veldt. It is a country perfectly flat, at a considerable elevation (5000 feet) above the sea level, destitute of anything approaching timber, or, indeed, of any sort of fuel save that left by grazing cattle. This *mest* (in Dutch)—*groslock*, we think, is the Scotch—gives, when dry, great heat, and burns rapidly. At Amersfort certain Boers of the real unadorned type called on us to try and sell horses. In this, dealing they could open their mouths well. There was some disappointment on their part, and angry remarks that, not content with taking their country, our men were actually picking up their cattle droppings. We think they finished by selling a horse or two, when the difficulty as to the method of payment arose.

No bank notes or cheques on the Standard Bank at Newcastle were to be accepted, but the hard money must be paid down then and there. We forgot how the affair was finally arranged, but fancy an English storekeeper came to the rescue. There is no denying the fact that these Boers have the greatest suspicion of Englishmen. That they have been plundered in their dealings with Jew, and probably not a few Scotch and English traders, to say nothing of German storekeepers there is no doubt. Many and curious are the anecdotes we have heard of the dodges resorted to by unscrupulous traders to victimize the ignorant Dutchman. One of these, which may be new to English readers, may be worth relating.

17

A certain Boer who had suspicions of a storekeeper's integrity with infinite labour made up by the help of a *Ready Reckoner* the value of so many waggon loads of wool which he was about to dispose of. The storekeeper's price fell much below that expected by the Boer. The latter triumphantly produced his book of figures to prove his correctness. The honest buyer was taken aback, but quickly recovered himself. Taking the *Ready Reckoner* from the Boer's hand, he looked at the title-page, and pointed out that the book was several years old, and that the multiplication there recorded was therefore valueless for the date at which the transaction took place. The Boer returned home serenely content. Probably finding the *Reckoner* dated before the Annexation, and the smaller price after, he is now riding with Joubert, and slaughtering prisoners, or some other equally inoffensive little game. Never mind, it's all the same, and some benevolent, but not very practical M.P.'s, will shield him, because, forsooth, a paper expressive of sympathy is being signed in Germany. We are rather far gone when we allow our neighbours to interfere in our treatment of our rebellious vassals.

The real object of a Boer s special aversion is the Hollander, that is, a native of Holland A few of these gentry are to be found in South Africa, and their superior education has enabled them to do a good stroke of business on the unsophisticated South African kinsmen. They are willing to turn their hands to any light employment where pickings are to be had, and generally occupy positions as schoolmasters or attorney or solicitor-generals. The Boer will admit that all Englishmen are not all rogues; but nothing on this earth will persuade him that a Hollander is not a person who has made his native country too hot for him. It may here be recorded that the Boers' notions of honesty are, by no means, strict Storekeepers have told us that their assistants always keep a watchful eye on their Dutch customers, who are apt to take away articles not paid for.

We remember a Jew shopkeeper in the Cape Colony detecting the theft of a pair of trousers. The Boer had got into a back room to try them on. He did so, and then pulled his own over them and marched out, saying, as he went by, that they did not fit. In these cases the dealer does not openly tax the customers with theft, but rather makes out a bill in which the missing articles are charged Often the Boers used to come into stores when our men were there, thinking, no doubt, that the blame of any missing articles would be charged to our Irregulars.

However, we will leave the Dutchmen for a while, they are quite able to take care of themselves, and continue our march across the High Veldt. This becomes extremely monotonous after a day or two. The same vast expanse of open arid plain unrelieved by landmark of any sort. Water scarce, and existing principally in small stagnant swamps. Occasionally a house might be seen in the far distance, with a willow or two planted in front, or we might pass a so called farm once in 24 hours. As a general rule, the whole location consists of an erection containing one, or at most two, rooms, A *kraal* of loose stones, some 3 or 4 feet high, for cattle completes the homestead. Wherein dwells some 12 or 15 Dutch, of ages varying from 3 months to many years. This we have heard described as a patriarchal mode of existence, it is certainly one very repugnant to English notions.

Let us give the narrative of a night's lodging at a Boer's house. Duty led us with an Irregular orderly past the house. It was night, and a great storm was gathering. We asked hospitality (and paid for it). Our horses were stripped and let out, and we came in in time for the evening meal. It consisted of goats' flesh, placed on the table in the pot it was boiled in. Every one dived and fished up with their own forks. There was a community in the matter of drinking apparatus, there being only two, both tin billys. Forks were scarce, and one used their own knives, grabbing in the pot for anything you wanted.

At an early hour two girls brought in a mysterious tin vessel with a small amount of water in it and a towel, and a very small one, too. This water was to wash every one's feet; the two daughters of the house did this, one washing, the other drying. As the family consisted of thirteen people, with two strangers, the state of water and towel when the operation was over may be left to the reader's imagination. He needs have a vivid one. Afterwards, with everything on save boots, we retired to roost. Will it be believed that the whole family—father, mother, grandmother, five sons, and four daughters, all grown up, together with any strangers that might happen to drop in—occupied the same chamber? and that a small one. There was but small delicacy observed. By the aid of a tallow candle, coats were taken off and rolled for pillows, and blankets came into use. The damsels were, by no means, careful to hide any of the charms that nature had provided them with.

Everyone slept where he happened to select. Save the fact that a recent fever was still hanging round us, and that the storm was raging fiercely, we should much have preferred the sky for a roof. As it was protected by our saddle, we fell asleep at last among the most diabolical concert from the snoring family it has ever been our misfortune to hear. This is the patriarchal mode of existence. We will answer that, if some of our humanitarian members slept one night such as this, he would forswear the cause of the Transvaal Boers. This man at whose house we slept owned 8000 acres of land. Occasionally we would purchase a fowl or two at these undesirable dwellings, but nether their occupants nor ourselves cared for much conversation. However, any sort of habitation broke the sameness of this country, which was also occasionally relieved by the view of large herds of *vildebeeste* and the various classes of *boks*. They would often approach in large numbers close to our line of march, which was pursued at a steady walk of 4 or 4½ miles an hour. Time being important, and ammunition valuable, the troop officers forbade any pursuit or firing, although, on our way south to the Zulu frontier two months later, a fair amount of sport was obtained.

Sept. 10. Reached the Vaal River and encamped. This was a red letter day for two reasons. First, on account of the stream, which, although very different from its appearance at Pniel and Klipdrift (Diamond Fields), is still a stream. That is, we could determine which way the current moved, a somewhat unusual circumstance in this flat country. We could bathe and wash, two luxuries beyond price. Then, in the next place, we had the pleasure of meeting a Dutch farmer belonging to the educated and enlightened section of the community. With Mr. Retief, his wife and handsome daughter, we spent half-an-hour very pleasantly. This gentleman is famous for being the son of the Dutch leader, who with his commando was treacherously murdered by Dingaan the Zulu king.

A massacre the Boers avenged to some purpose at a later date. In their earlier conflicts with the Zulus, the Boers seemed to have displayed a bravery amounting at times to recklessness. Men, women, and children alike took part in the struggle, which ended in the division of the Zulu nation, and a disastrous defeat of the anti-Boer party. That this spirit exists in some of the present generation of Boers, cannot be denied, although the later history of the South African Republic show a lamentable falling off in patriotism and self-sacrifice. Those who were acquainted with Mr. Piet Uys and his sons, killed on the Zlobane, March 28, 1879, will bear testimony to their courage and devotion.

Sir Evelyn Wood, we believe, looked upon Mr. Piet Uys as a most valuable friend and ally, and had good reason to lament his untimely death. We forget how many sons this brave man left behind; but let us hope the Imperial Government did not forget its obligations, and that they are now ranked on our side in the present struggle. The *landroost* of Utrecht, Mr. Rudolph and his brother Andries were also prominent at the Zulu War. Of the latter it was said, he could see a native at a mile distance, and shoot him at two. Allowing for hyperbole, we can of our own knowledge speak of their wonderful powers of vision and of their accuracy as marksmen.

In the first qualification they hold their own with the natives. Cornelius Uys could distinguish objects with the naked eye, as well as we could with a field glass. He could with his Lancaster rifle bring down birds on the wing in a truly sportsmanlike manner. Of Andries Rudolph, Piet Uys used to say, "Rudolph no very quick, but he shoot straight." All these men, and all the best and bravest of the Transvaal will be on our side in the struggle. Let us hope their uncultured brethren will not murder them for their attachment to English rule. The Boers are merely fighting, because they hate us, who buy their land, develop their country, and do not let them whip their own niggers at will.

To return to Mr. Retief, we regret we were unable to have a longer interview with him. He had a well built and comfortably furnished house, with orchard, and out-buildings, and enclosures, that did one's heart good to look at, after three or four days' journey over the High Veldt. At parting he requested us to send him a schoolmaster, should we meet with that article in our travels. We think all classes of Dutchmen recognise the value of education for their children, although but few incur the expense of a teacher. In the Transvaal indeed, a very small percentage of the farmers have accommodation for a schoolmaster, were they even willing to spare the small charge made by this person, who is generally a wanderer with whom other callings have proved failures.

Sept. 14. Four days more of the High Veldt, and we reach Nazareth, or as the English call it Middleburg. The former name were better retained to avoid complication with the Middleburg of the Cape Colony, which is the chief place of a division almost wholly inhabited by the Dutch. Of Nazareth we saw but little, as the next day but one we marched. The intervening Sunday was fully occupied in fitting out the troops with such supplies as could be procured in the village.

It boasted of a small street or two, planted with willows, a post office, and some grog shops, called canteens or hotels, where everything that was poisonous in the way of liquor was retailed at famine prices. The following day saw us encamped on the Steelport River, of which we were destined to see a good deal before relinquishing our attack on Secocoeni.

Sept 19. Reached the Leydenberg flats and camped some 5 or 6 miles from the town. No more high veldt but steep barren mountains on every side. We here discovered our proximity to the enemy's country—a deserted farm lying about a mile off, visited, however, in the day time by its owner, who had trekked into Leydenberg.

Sept 20. Marched into Leydenberg. Time occupied from Pietermaritzburg 23 days, of which we halted four. The distance supposed 380 miles. We had, however, diverged from the direct route. Somebody said our guide led us astray on purpose, to visit a sweetheart at a Dutchman's farm; but, however, that might be, we certainly got over 400 miles in 19 days, a performance of which we were not a little proud. The hills must have been rather frequent, for we had climbed 3500 feet from Pietermaritzburg.

Leydenberg is a pretty town with abundance of trees and watercourses. The Standard Bank of British South Africa has a branch here, although, we believe business is very slack since the cessation of work at the gold fields, close by. The town, which was previously the centre of a republic of its own, before being incorporated with the Transvaal, has shops with the usual inferior goods at unheard of prices. The rate of transport from Durban at this time was 40s. per 100 lbs., a fact that storekeepers did not fail to make the most of. As a waggon carries from 6000 to 8000 lbs., the owner of one waggon could make some £120 to £160, for the up journey, and have the down journey as well. The latter would probably clear his few expenses and replace any bullocks he might happen to loose. This is most certainly the way to make money, but the labour is intense. The Government load for waggons is 4500 lbs., but their oxen are not so well looked after as the transport riders are.

Our transactions at the shop consisted in purchasing tobacco at 7s. per lb., and one bottle of beer at 5s. 6d. The ordinary price of this tamarind tobacco is 3s., and of beer at Durban 1s. 6d., which allows a fair margin for profit. These people did not, in the least, object to fleecing we poor soldiers who had come to rid them of their bugbear,

Secocoeni.

From Leydenberg to Delagoa Bay is, we believe, 140 miles. There is no doubt but that under a settled Government the place will develop. The road to the coast after crossing the Lembombo divide becomes desperately unhealthy. Travellers during nine months of the year being attacked by fevers of virulent and fatal character. The *tetse* fly also prevents the use of oxen and horses for draught purposes. This fly lives in the bush, and attacks horse and oxen, stinging them; one bite is enough, and they waste and died the next rain. It is harmless to man. One firm of merchants endeavoured to organize a camel train, but the result was a failure.

A railway will ultimately be constructed, the Portuguese Government having expressed its willingness to find money. The graziers and grain producers of the Northern part of the Transvaal will thus procure a ready means of forwarding their wool, hides, and com to the best harbour of South Africa. This railway would no doubt have been started before but for the most determined opposition of the colonists of Natal. The Natal Government levy taxes and customs on all things disembarked at Durban for the Transvaal. Their roads are full of Transvaal produce; their inns of Transvaal people. Therefore they oppose it.

By this railway Natal would loose half its revenue; more than half, in fact. They oppose Confederation, because the common sense of a united assembly would trample on the meanness thus perpetrated. This railway to Leydenberg from Delagoa Bay would save a journey of five months at least, and would reduce the cost of all things. By taking European produce, and consequently English tradesmen, into the country, it would do more to pacify the Transvaal than all the troops we now are sending out. Then the trade into the vast interior would be increased tenfold, and civilization with it.

The Colonial Office, no doubt, knows this, and probably the scheme will be taken in hand by them to some purpose. It is far better to come from them than from any of the Colonial Governments, who would only make a party matter of the affair.

The gold fields at Leydenberg are played out; there never was alluvial or riverbed gold, only pockets in the hills where the trains of many centuries had washed it into fissures of the rocks. It never payed particularly well, and there is no doubt it will soon die out. Old Australian diggers were woefully disappointed with it. Leydenberg must then turn to its proper use—a depot for the interior markets.

CHAPTER 3

Secocoeni's War

Sept 21. Left this outpost of civilisation early on our advance to Fort-Burgers. The track resembled the bed of a mountain torrent more than anything else, and led along the foot of rugged hills whose slopes were covered with a dense growth of thorn bushes. The heat now became oppressive, and henceforth we were dependent for water on the rivers Spekboom and Steelport; of other supply during our operations we saw none. Fort-Burgers is situated at the confluence of these two rivers, and is surrounded by the usual barren hills and dense thorn.

Of the operations under Col. Rowlands, V.C., it is not our purpose here to speak. The force at his disposal was quite inadequate to approach Secocoeni's town even had we been supplied with water. The sufferings of the 13th Light Infantry on their march were painful to witness, and Colonel Rowlands might well say the game was not worth the candle.

Hostilities consisted in marching under a broiling sun at the foot of steep mountains, whence the Basutos fired with such weapons and skill as they were possessed of. Fortunately the damages were small. In the words of one of our men in the Zulu War, "This is different to Secocoeni's, where they used to come down and fire a bucket of powder and a bag of bullets at us without hitting, and then go away to bed."

Why President Burgers got into a conflict about such a hopeless country is more than we can discover. Moreover, when he was in it he and his Boers failed lamentably in their attack. The Dutchmen showed a great want of alacrity in joining their commandoes. What fighting took place was done chiefly by English and German mercenaries; and, on the whole, Mr. Burgers (who by the way is a clergyman by profession) did not shine as a military leader or war minister.

To add to our troubles, horse sickness declared itself in one corps, in the first week of October. Of this disease I know no remedy, neither did Mr. Duck of the Royal Artillery, our veterinary surgeon, ever discover any. This officer had ample scope for studying the symptoms of this scourge, which carried off its victims in periods, varying from four to twenty-four hours. The symptoms are, heaving in the flanks, horse alternately lies down and rises every five minutes. The last falls to the ground are accompanied by a profuse discharge of white frothy matter from the nose. The only precautions we could adopt were to draw away the dead animal immediately, burn the head collar, and bury the usual discharge. Latterly, the deaths were 8 or 10 *per diem*. Every cavalry officer will imagine the feelings with which we saw disappear, the poor animals that had marched with us so many hundred of miles, since the formation of the corps.

These horses were mostly bred in the Stormberg a very extensive district of the Cape Colony between Queenstown and Dordrecht. The average price was £22. Those that survived the dangers of the previous campaign were invaluable, though not much to look at. They were short hardy horses, 14.3, or thereabouts, inured to short rations and other privations. The breed of horses in South Africa is deteriorating year by year, the farmers from increased attention to ostrich farming and other causes, neglecting the horse. In former times Cape horses were well known in India, now the whalers or Australian horses have taken their place. In the Zulu War at a later date, when alongside the K.D.G's. and 17th Lancers, we congratulated ourselves on not being mounted on English horses, the majority of whom gave way under the hardships of the campaign.

At the same time it would be out of the question to mount an English cavalry regiment in South Africa, as there is necessarily a limit to even what the Cape horse will carry. We regret we never inquired during the war what weight a lancer's horse carried. Sword, lance, carbine, 100 rounds of ammunition, blankets, picket pegs, with valise and cloak, in addition to the trooper, made up a weight most distressing and inconvenient. To return to the horse sickness, I have heard that the Boers have a nostrum which cures horses in the earlier stages. It was not, however, to their interest to cure ours, as we had of course to procure fresh ones, which meant a ready sale for theirs. They, the Boers, occasionally bring forward a so-called "salted" horse, that is, one which has had the sickness and recovered.

They say that a horse can never be attacked a second time. On

25

this account sums of £70 to £100, are demanded for these animals, a portion of the price to lie over till the immunity from disease of the horse becomes an established fact. We do not know how this arrangement works. On the 13th October, whilst a portion of corps was patrolling the gold fields, the regiment received orders through its commanding officer Capt. Watt Whalley, from Colonel Rowlands, to remove bag and baggage and rejoin Colonel Buller, and march to Newcastle. At that time we had lost 47 horses since our entrance to the Transvaal through sickness, besides those killed in action. We felt much sympathy with Colonel Rowlands, who saw himself beaten out of the country by causes utterly beyond his control. Two British regiments, with several thousand native auxiliaries, and a good transport train and commissariat department were required by Sir Garnet to get possession of Secocoeni's stronghold, and water, when Sir Garnet was there was plentiful.

We arrived in Leydenberg on the 3rd inst. with the headquarters, and a large train of ox-waggons having taken a westerly and better track along the Waterfall valley to return with. There are several farms (then deserted) on this road, with a tropical vegetation in the valley, and, I fancy, the inseparable fever. One of our Dutch waggon drivers owned one of these farms, and he complained bitterly of his hard lot. As his ramshackle waggons were earning £1 10s. a day each, with a load not to exceed 3000 (the usual one is 8000), we could not give him much sympathy. The day after our arrival, whilst getting ready for our march southward, we were surprised by an order to saddle up one hundred men, and return with all speed to Colonel Rowlands. The colonel meditated giving the natives a gentle reminder before leaving them. The business in question related to a *stad* (camp) on the other side of the Steelport in a strong position on high ground, commanded by still higher mountains. This was stormed by the 13th Light Infantry and some native allies in first-class style. Although the loss in killed and wounded to that gallant corps was not great, the whole affair was most creditable to all parties concerned.

We had many a march with the 13th before leaving Africa, and a finer body of officers and men it has never been our lot to have for neighbours. With a year or two more of War Office reforms, we suppose that this famous regiment will also be one of the skeletons, reminding one by its numbers only, if perchance even that escape, of what an English regiment had been. They have been called on, and that too nearly the moment they returned, to furnish volunteers for service in India. Since then they have been again stripped till but few old Africans are in their ranks. After this attack on Tolyana (we think that was the name), we fled southward with our utmost speed. We marched seventy miles in two days, Captain Whalley thinking to save what could be saved of the remainder of our horses.

On Nov. 4 we drew rein on the shore of Lake Chrassie, a pool of stagnant water, useless alike for ablution or drinking. It covers 100 acres, with a depth of about 18 inches. We passed several decent farms on this route, which was to the eastward of that we had previously used. One of them was pointed out to us as belonging to a Boer who had been fined £100 for cowardice in the matter of the commandoes against Secocoeni. We do not know if it was paid or not. Most of these Boers were supposed to be friendly. In fact, we are convinced that all of those with good houses, homesteads, and a stake in the country of any magnitude think in their heart of hearts, that British rule is a desirable one, an improvement on the bankrupt anarchy of the South African Republic,

A more lamentable state of affairs than that existing in the South African Republic before the annexation cannot be conceived. The President, before departing, gave in his final address a very accurate picture of things as they were. He evidently considered the case quite hopeless. The complete demoralisation can be best summed up by saying, as, indeed, President Burgers said plainly:

> The native enemies were taking possession of the soil of the Republic, and that there was not a Boer who would fight, neither was there a sovereign in the exchequer of the state.

On Nov. 7 we camped on the Vaal River. Here dwelt one Buhrmann, an enlightened Boer, with a solid stone house, outbuilding, and orchards. All this man's family spoke perfect English, probably the younger ones knew but little Dutch. Their education had, moreover, taught them to exercise considerable acuteness in matters of business, and to open their mouths widely. The following day we encamped on a nearly stagnant stream, at a place called Robertson, after two Scotch brothers, who have there large stores and an ostrich enclosure.

Several days' halt was made to take stock of deficient equipment; and one day was occupied by all the officers in roaming through the country looking for newly-purchased horses which had strayed. On this day we called at several Dutch farms mostly showing signs of indolence or poverty. We were everywhere received with civility, and every information given us. This, it must be remembered, was antecedent to the Zulu War, which was expected to break out every day.

Consequently our temporizing Dutch neighbours saw it was their interest to treat us with consideration. On the 20th Nov. we arrived at Wakkerstrom, or Wesselstrom, a neat little village, that will someday rise to be a town of importance. Two days later we marched to the position we were to occupy at Eland's Neck, till the war broke out. It is midway between Utrecht and Wakkerstrom 16 miles from either.

This concludes a record of over a thousand miles of travel and march.

CHAPTER 4

Zlobane & Beyond

On the 10th of March, 1879, we found ourselves on that most uncomfortable of vehicles a Natal post-cart, *en route* from Durban for Estcourt. We were there to join a detachment of Irregular Horse. They were on their march to join Wood's column then at Kambula. Between the jolts one had time to speculate on what manner of men we had the task of marching some 200 miles of country with. One previous experience of newly raised volunteers had, we are bound to say, prejudiced us most strongly against them: they appeared to be rough, undisciplined and disrespectful to their officers, fearfully slovenly and the veriest drunkards and winebibbers that ever took carbine in hand.

On the other hand they looked, what they eventually were, just the rough and hardy men to wage a partisan warfare against an active enemy. The steeds they bestrode were as hardy as themselves. In short, they were the makings of a rough but effective force, could they ever be brought into anything like order. It needed a thoroughly masterful man, like Colonel Redvers Buller, to bring these desperadoes into subjection. After a dusty and uncomfortable journey we reached P.M.B., as the Natalians love to call Pietermaritzburg, at six. Seven found us at dinner in the Royal Hotel, a good one for Natal. We were detained a day at Maritzburg, and on the 12th of March left it by post-cart.

This 12th of March was the day set apart for a day of humiliation by the governor: all shops were closed and business totally suspended. The people of P.M.B. did not look as humiliated as they ought to be, in fact the day was gone by for that: most of them thought it a bore, others took advantage of a holiday and a fine day, and went on picnics. The danger of invasion which had lain on the country so long was just lifting. The first of a great series of reinforcements had arrived; the

29

Shah had landed her Naval Brigade and her St. Helena garrison; the *Tamar* had landed the 57th, brought from Ceylon; and the telegram flashed the number of regiments already more than half way on their voyage.

To return to our journey; just outside the town came the awful town hill, up whose steep sides, in wet weather it takes a week for bullocks to climb the five miles. At all the stiff pulls we had to get out and trudge behind the cart, for though the post-cart proprietors covenant to deliver your body in a more or less battered condition to your destination, the unlucky traveller finds that a considerable portion of the way must be compassed on his own supporters. After a weary climb we reached the hill top, and then scrambling on to our perches we held on by the skin of our teeth and our eyelids to the slipping mailbags on which we sit. While we tear down the gentle slope that stretches to Howick, we can glance at what a Natal post-cart is like. Imagine then a square box perched on two strong wheels, the paint antediluvian at least and of a dingy red, very roughly made, very strong and elastic.

The horses are six in number, wild, untrained, matched on undiscoverable principles, wheeler one day, leader next. The driver a half caste, generally looking more or less demoniacal in voice and features, when, urging on his horses already galloping freely, he stands up in the swaying vehicle and plies his long whip with fierce yells. The horses are arrayed in harness that would make a London saddler stare, it consists of breast-strap, instead of collar and traces; it is much showier both in the team driven the stage into and out of any town. The travellers, one sits on either side of the driver in a sort of pill box much too small for them, the driver's box is raised six inches or so, the people on the back-seat, two or three in number, all perched on the top of the mailbags; they cling with desperate energy but feel utterly helpless and at the mercy of their driver. The pace is a good gallop at all times.

Arrived at Howick, we lunched and then strolled out to see the waterfall of the Umgemi River, which is certainly a grand spectacle, the water plunges some 350 feet sheer down into a pool below, a dense spray rises to a considerable height from the pool and rare and beautiful ferns clothe the sides of the chasm; on this occasion the volume of water was not large. The ford is just above the fall, and instances of whole waggons and teams being washed over are told.

Towards night we reached a hut by the wayside, dignified by the name of hotel and called Currie's Post, here we were to pass the night.

This we did in a double-bedded room, the occupant of the other bed was a Dutchman, who said he had not been in bed for a week, his snores presently proved his assertions. Remonstrances were totally unavailing, light cavalry in the shape of boots and brushes were equally ineffectual, heavy dragoons in the form of a carpet bag also useless. At last we had to drag our aching frame, black and blue from the jolting, across the room, shaking and severer measures failed to in any way disturb him, and finding it utterly useless had to leave him to sleep the sleep of the just.

At six we again started and breakfasted, after some few miles, at Weston or Mooi River; we reached Estcourt at three. The road in places is simply fearful, a hill side near Karkloof especially bad. One shuddered as the thought of the dreadful sufferings of the wounded flashed across you. Their agony as they had to pass over any road in Natal must have been awful. They are totally at the mercy of the drivers of ambulances, mostly some cold blooded Hottentot, and in spite of every exertion the doctors or the men of the Army Hospital Corps can make, they must feel the roads terribly.

At Estcourt we found our detachment encamped, and directly afterwards several hundred horses passed through on their way from the Orange River Free State, where they were bought, to Maritzburg. We promptly acted on our authority from the Remount Committee, and mounted the detachment. The mode of selection was primitive in the extreme; the horses were driven into a stone enclosure, called a *kraal*, every man then went in with a halter and from the plunging and kicking mass selected what suited himself. The result being with men who did not know about horses absurd, some large men got small horses and *vice versa*; this was soon rectified. The knowing ones got ponies as a rule, short, wiry, and thick little brutes that could wear down any big horse by sheer dint of superior powers of endurance. The best colour to take was bay or brown, as grey horses afford a much better target than either of these two colours.

The next few days were most fearfully busy, and what with getting men's names, list of stores, getting men's regimental numbers and making them undergo a thorough medical inspection, not much time was to spare; then the horses had to be shod, branded, hoof-marked and saddles fitted on. The men, many of them knowing little about riding, had to be taught; they learnt by dint of falling off, and at last managed to stick on well enough. The falls were many, as riders were bad and horses young and untaught. The men entered into their new duties

31

with all sailors' heartiness, and were very glad to be at last mounted, as they had had a long weary march from Durban up the dusty roads. The events of the next fortnight would be needless to particularize.

It would interest no one to know the various duties performed and the country passed over. We will merely say that the whole of Natal, except the coast-belt, is a succession of treeless terraced plateaux. The towns, so called, consist of a church, two public-houses, a police station, laager and a couple of stores, where the prices charged were more or less extortionate. At Colenso, where there is a fine iron bridge, complete in all but two arches, over the Tugela, we had the misfortune to camp on bad ground; a fearful thunderstorm came on, and we did not awake until a small but lively river began to trickle down our back; on lighting a candle the sight that met our eyes did not cheer us; our clothes were wet through, provisions *ditto*, ourselves as bad: we had eventually to collect and make a pile of everything and sat till morning on the table, a gruesome spectacle.

At Newcastle, Sir Bartle Frere, passing us on his way to Pretoria, addressed the men, wishing them, in answer to their hearty cheers, every success. The High Commissioner himself travelled in a rough mule waggon, and it was not saying a little for his zeal and determination when he took such a long journey, with a possibility of maltreatment at the hands of the Boers to crown all. A few days previously we had passed Sir Theophilus Shepstone sitting in a like conveyance, eating his frugal dinner while the mules grazed around, and contemplating a fearful hill he had to ascend with the most disconsolate looks.

Next Utrecht, in the Transvaal, was reached, all the inhabitants were in laager here every night, and a complete panic prevailed among the towns-people. The *laager* was garrisoned by the 4th Bang's Own under Colonel Bray. The first field hospital for Wood's column was here.

In the proper sequence of events the actions at Kambula and Zlobane should next be recorded. As they have been so frequently described in recent works they shall be briefly dismissed. At this time Ekowe was in the act of being relieved by Lord Chelmsford. For that purpose he was to advance from the Tugela. General Wood received orders to make a diversion by attacking the Zlobane mountain. At that time he was encamped at Kambula Kop, about twenty-three miles from the Zlobane. This mountain was deemed to be impregnable by the Zulus. It was a huge square mountain, with rocky precipitous sides with a flat top some four or five miles long, and of a good breadth.

There was only one way up which was hard and difficult, and at the other end there was a way down, but it was well-nigh impracticable. Possibly there may have been unknown cattle paths down its side. Colonel Buller set out to attack this on the 27th of March, with 400 mounted men from Kambula and the posts round, and some native allies. He reached after a long ride the foot of the Zlobane about night fall, riding on after dark and changing his position so as to avoid being surprised in the night. The night was gloomy and damp.

At dawn the next morning everyone was up and ready early. The colonel was no man for delay, and at once advanced. The end of the mountain where the road up lies, was the place selected for attack. Here the enemy was in force. A round knoll rose at the foot of, but detached from, the mountain. The enemy lined the rocks of the mountain side. Colonel Buller sent two troops to the top of the mound or knoll. Under cover of their fire the attack was delivered, the hill taken in good form by the Irregulars, leading their horses up the steep sides, and thus the hitherto impregnable mountain was taken. It was so far a very gallant affair. Arrived at the top the men scattered and fired at their foes below them in the rocks.

Captain the Baron von Steitenkvon was here shot as he was leaning over the edge of the hill. It is well to cut a painful story short. By a most extraordinary chance the picked Zulu army was on its way to attack Kambula. It heard the firing, diverged, and was seen in the distance. History says, some mistake as to placing the *videttes* took place, but not by any one under Col. Buller's orders. However, that may be, it is no use opening up old wounds. To retreat down the road that the mountain was ascended by was impossible. The only way was to move along the top of the hill, and chance getting down at the other end. General Wood who had been coming to see how the operations went on, had Captain the Hon. Ronald Campbell, one of his staff, killed.

Captain Barton of the Coldstream Guards, serving with the Irregulars, went to bury his body with a small troop of the Frontier Light Horse. Caught by the advancing wave of Zulus, they were never again seen alive. Colonel Weatherley was with the whole of his corps, save seven men, killed. All his officers, and his son, a boy of fifteen, fell by his side. Piet Uys, the brave Dutch farmer fell, and many more Irregulars, at various places. At the end of the mountain the descent was fearful, and the causalities great. The men led their horses down as well as they could. The Zulus who had retired into the rocks on the mountains being stormed, now reappeared, followed along the hill and closed up.

The havoc was dire, and save for the heroic efforts of Colonel Buller would have been extermination. Six lives he is known to have saved that day personally, how many more by his orders and example, it would be impossible to tell. Major Knox Leet of the 13th Lt. Infantry, serving with some native allies, brought off Lieut. Smith of the Frontier Light Horse, on a pack horse—his own was shot—and earned the V.C. Some of the Light Horse kept in some measure the advancing Zulus back, and enabled the rear-guard to extricate themselves. The mounted Infantry ought to have been here to support the Irregulars, and keep down the fire, while they descended the hill. However, orders were sent to them, and were either ill delivered or misunderstood, for instead of being in position on the neck leading down from the Zlobane, they were on the Zinguin neck

The main body under Colonel Buller having managed to extricate themselves from the defile, leaving many dead behind, pursued their way. The great army of the Zulus did not come within shot of this body. However, the two or three thousand of the enemy who had occupied the Zlobane, and who had been beaten in the morning followed them, and for miles the fight continued. Many officers and men fell, Lieut. Williams and Potter of the Regulars, and it was late before the broken Irregulars reached camp utterly crushed. The only bright spot to remember, is the heroic courage of Col. Buller, Major Knox Leet, Captain Cecil D'arcy of the Light Horse and others. Capt. D'arcy received the V.C. at Ulundi; but deserved it often at Zlobane. The camp was found entrenched by General Wood who surely foresaw the morrow's attack. The butcher's bill was a heavy one that night, and adjutants had difficulty in making it out. The losses in horses was large, and the Cavalry of Wood's column was for the time paralyzed. Now for the bright side of the picture.

Early next morning General Wood received intelligence from a native, that the Zulus had left Zlobane and were marching to attack him. Two companies who had gone to the neighbouring hills woodcutting were recalled, and about noon came in. At the same time an immense mass of Zulus were seen to emerge from near the Zinguin neck, and advance steadily towards Kambula. They come very steadily on in regular formation. As they passed a broad track was made through the long grass, which was completely destroyed. Their numbers were estimated at 25,000 men. The Basutos, who had stuck like leeches to the cattle on the Zlobane the day before and brought them off safely, left the *laager* and refused to stay.

Through the, fight they hovered round the flank of the Zulus firing continually. The position at Kambula was at the end of a long peninsula of a hill if we may call it so. The fortifications were three in number, and were at the three angles of an equilateral triangle. The first which was garrisoned by some of the 13th and 90th L.I., was on the highest point, it was of earth faced with stone. Here General Wood commanded. Down a gentle slope was the *laager*, it was formed of waggons placed in a square: sods were placed round the waggons up to a level of the axle trees, and again above on the top. Two tiers of fire could thus be obtained.

On the side nearest the fort, the 90th and 13th were, on the right more of the 90th, the third side was held by Irregulars, and the fourth by the 13th and 90th again. This laager contained all the horses, and the hospital. The horses were attached to picket lines. The last defence was likewise a *laager*, but contained the transport oxen. It was much smaller, and held by one company of the 13th. Between the fort, as the little round stone entrenchment was called, and the *laager*, the guns were placed, four in number. Two more were close to the fort, they were mountain guns, one got disabled early in the fight. On the right the ground rose abruptly from the plain below. To the front it was level on the *plateau* at the hill top. On the left just under the cattle laager there was a *krantz* or precipice, on the rear the ground sloped gradually.

Some mounted troops sallied out to draw on the enemy. General Wood wished to irritate the Zulus into attacking on one side before the other, in other words to beat them: in detail. It succeeded. After exchanging shots the mounted troops retired to the *laager*. Lieut. Browne of the 24th, serving with Mounted Infantry earned a V.C. by rescuing a man whose horse was shot. The right side was attacked about one by the enemy, who were received with such a tremendous volley by the 90th that they never again attacked that face. They had more cover on all the other sides, and availed themselves of it. The fighting was now fast and furious, attacks being delivered time after time by the enemy, who advanced with the greatest gallantry. They were very badly off for provisions, and actually ate some provisions of the Irregulars under a hot fire.

The tents had of course been struck, but as some of the men had been getting their dinner when the alarm sounded, some of the provisions were outside. The enemy took advantage of any cover there was about, to annoy by a hot fire. They then used to gather and make a gallant rush. Availing themselves of the precipice under the cattle *laager*, they took that position and the garrison had to retire to the other. Two companies of the 90th tried to retake under Major Hackett, they, however, had to retreat with their leader most fearfully wounded. About half-past four some of the 13th, and some Irregular Volunteers under Raaf, left the horse *laager*, and advanced to the edge of the precipice by Col. Buller's order. They took the Zulus in the flank and firing down the precipice killed numbers till forced to retire. Colonel Buller commanded in the laager. The artillery was fought well and was in the open between the laager and the fort.

The greatest loss came from some rocks some 1200 yards off, from whence the enemy kept up a galling fire. Two men were especially good shots, brothers they were said to be when found dead afterwards with a pile of empty cartridges beside them. The great question now was, would ammunition hold out, the attack had been so desperate and prolonged, that it was for hours a tossup who would win. It showed no falling off as yet. It was lucky two such exceptional regiments as the 13th and 90th were engaged. The result even in the hands of General Wood, might have been different, had two boy regiments been engaged. Towards five a shiver seemed to run through the enemy, and all in a moment they broke and fled. Umbeline had led them gallantly the whole day, rumour said he was now wounded. The broken relics of the Irregular horse now sallied out in pursuit. The horses were so thoroughly done up by the fatigues of the previous day, that the pursuit was not so ruinous as it would otherwise have been.

Nevertheless under the vigorous direction of Colonel Buller, it was well sustained till nightfall. The enemy were so exhausted that they made no fight of it, but were shot down. However they had sent away all the Zlobane cattle which they had recaptured early in the fight. Night fell on the scattered fugitives and saved them. The Irregulars returned. In this battle the Zulus lost at least 2500 men. It was by far the hardest of the war, and coming as it did on two defeats, Isandula and Zlobane, raised the spirits of the soldiers enormously. From that hour General Wood and Colonel Buller possessed in even a greater degree, the unbounded confidence of their troops. That battle saved the Transvaal from a Zulu invasion. If it had been lost the Boers would have been annihilated.

CHAPTER 5

Pursuing the Zulus

Our next duty was to convey the wounded from Kambula down to the nearest hospital at Utrecht; a most tedious and at the same time truly fearful task The roads, or rather tracks, were terribly rough and full of holes, the ambulances very carelessly driven, in spite of the efforts of the doctors. With the first convoy a halt had to be made on the banks, of the Blood River, which was in high flood. The Blood River divides the Transvaal and Zululand, it is so called from a battle between the Boers and Zulus when the river ran blood from the quantity of slain. The flood was so high waggons could not cross, ambulances had to be sent for from Balte Spruit on the opposite side; they arrived at ten p.m., a light span bridge was thrown across the river by a company of the 13th regiment, and the camp entrenched for the night.

A most miserable night was then passed by the Irregulars who had crossed to the opposite bank, the swamp was four inches deep in water, mosquitoes aggressive in the extreme—the only way to rest was to lean against the waggon wheel. Towards day the bridge, which had been broken by the force of the current during the night, was repaired. The sick and wounded were transferred across the stream, they then had to be carried through the worst part of the swamp to the waggons some quarter of a mile off. The waggons could not get nearer, the ground being too soft.

The sufferings of the wounded must have been extreme, as they were carried in *dhoolys* over the rough ground and through deep pools. It was curious to observe the difference in men, thus equally suffering; some never uttered a sound; others groaned most horribly; some only expressed fierce anxiety to be getting on; others were sunk in profound apathy and seemed utterly indifferent to all around them.

As we proceeded, we often had to halt to administer brandy to some poor fellows who were sinking, and once or twice to find that some of the number had breathed his last, in spite of all the care that under such circumstances could be given to them. One in particular I remember, a poor old soldier of twenty-eight years' service, he had been wounded at Kambula and had sank under the awful sufferings incidental to such a journey. At last we reached Balte Spruit, and were glad to get rest, having been twenty-four hours without food. The next day we escorted the wounded a few miles on the road to Utrecht, and were met by a fresh escort to whom we handed them over.

A day or two later we joined Wood's column at Kambula, having escorted ammunition to replace that expended in the fight of the 29th. Our next duty was a patrol to Luneberg in the Transvaal to convey despatches; this was an entirely new part of the country to us. It was a long barren ride, having been raided through repeatedly by the enemy under Umbeline, a savage chief of freebooters. Near here Moriarty's party of the 80th had been cut off on the Intombi River, a tributary of the Pongola, Luneberg itself is inhabited principally by German settlers, it is built round a mission station. It has the usual stores and a Lutheran church. We were most hospitably received by the small garrison, who were most anxious for the news of the fights of the 28th and 29th of March.

We were quartered for the night in the Lutheran church; tired out with our long ride we selected each the most comfortable of the pews and fell asleep, nor was it till roused by the voices of the congregation singing Luther's morning hymn that we awoke. The people, with true German kindliness, knowing how tired we were, had let us sleep on. At first we did not know where we were and rubbed our eyes in surprise, affording a most edifying spectacle. It was really ludicrous to see the troopers who slept some distance down gradually awakening, whilst red nightcaps began to bob up one by one over the level of the pews. The expression of their faces were various and amusing as the hymn pealed out all around them; one, in particular, making frantic exertions to conceal a goose he had killed a mile or two outside the town on the previous day, and which he feared some thrifty housewife would recognise, looked particularly sheepish. We returned by way of Utrecht and reached Kambula without further adventure.

The next few days passed without special incident. The detachment of our corps at Kambula amounted to 170 men with some 150 horses, but the greater portion were completely done up with constant patrols and the retreat from Zlobane. Our duties consisted of the usual regimental guards, cattle-guards, *vedettes*, night pickets, patrols, but the worst duty of all was the wood-fatigue. The nearest wood was some six miles off on the summit of a mountain. We had to go every day with the infantry, to cut and carry it. It grew among huge rocks, and it was hard work to keep the men at their various duties, some throwing down, others carrying, some cutting and carrying it to the waggons some quarter of a mile off, more again loading it up. The huge rocks gave the men excellent opportunities of skulking, of which they often availed themselves; it required all your energies to keep them at their work.

The captain of infantry who commanded the united party had orders to report any officer, sitting down even, to General Wood; and however much the general was liked, no one desired a personal interview with him when he had to speak about a neglect of duty. The wood was principally used in the bakery which was always kept going. The daily ration of wood per man was only three pounds, which was afterwards reduced to one pound, this to cook everything but bread; the men, however, managed to make out with cow-dung, which they collected, dried, and used as fuel.

On the 16th of April, while escorting waggons to Balte Spruit, a survivor of Zlobane was discovered, a trooper, Grandier of Weatherley's Border Horse; he had been captured on the 28th of March and taken to Ulundi, as he said, though it must have been some other *kraal* as his description did not tally with that of Ulundi. He had been sent back to Umbeline's people for torture, but had managed to kill one of his guards, the other running away. Grandier was in a fearful state when found, naked, thin, and almost dying of exhaustion. He said that a day or two before the whole Zulu Army had passed within a short distance on their return march to the Royal Kraal. They had evidently recruited at Zlobane after their defeat. He was promptly cared for, Umbeline had been shot some few days previous by the hand of Captain Prior of the 80th regiment, after a long chase of some twelve miles; Umbeline who was certainly one of the most dashing of all the Zulu generals, was a Swazi by birth; he was the very man to carry out those guerilla tactics that the Zulus ought to have relied on for success.

The kits of the officers who fell at Zlobane and Kambula were sold about this time, the prices realised were enormous—tins of preserved meat which are sold at home for one shilling, here realized six shillings, matches as high in price as ninepence per box. Cigars and tobacco made fabulous prices, indeed one was almost tempted to think how much our individual kits would have made. It was almost worth while being shot just to try.

We went down on escort to Utrecht for a day, and there saw and interviewed Oham, a brother of Ketchwayo who had surrendered some time before, and the fetching away of whom from the heart of the Zulu country had been one of the most brilliant feats of the whole war. It was carried out under the direction of Colonel Buller; Oham and several attendants and wives were brought out by a bold dash. An absurd scene occurred crossing one of the rivers, two of Oham's wives were or pretended to be afraid of the water, two troopers were therefore told off to take the ladies on their backs and swim over; one finding her cavalier rather knocking up in the transit, quickly dived off and swam like a duck to the shore, immediately the other followed suit and both reached the bank leaving their bearers struggling in the stream, to be received on gaining the bank by the unmerciful laughter of their comrades.

To add insult to injury the fair ladies addressed them in Zulu, which the interpreter translated to be "Him no good," a salutation which did not check the laughter. Poor ladies, they were not treated very chivalrously, for on Oham being driven in General Wood's trap to Utrecht, he complained very much of an iron rail that ran round the seat, so two ladies were put up and used as cushions, their lord sitting in their lap, no light infliction for them as he weighed some twenty honest stone. The way Oham used to knock about his attendants gave one some sort of idea how absolute the Zulu king and chiefs must be; for the slightest offence the unhappy servant got a bang with a *knobk-errie* on the head that bowled him over like a ninepin.

Apropos of Oham, an officer who shared a tent with two others was shot or died of fever at Ekowe, among his things was a tinned ham, the two other officers who messed with him having frugal minds resolved, as prices were fearfully high, to sell the ham. It realized forty-five shillings which went to the mess account of the three. The heliograph that afternoon flashed the news to Ekowe that Oham had surrendered; one of the two survivors burst into his tent where his comrade slept with the news. His comrade enjoying his afternoon *siesta* only caught the word Oham, and something about being taken. "What," said he, "another ham, how jolly!" regret for his dead comrade struggling against his joy at the supposed discovery of another treasure. We fancy Oham had an idea that he would be made by us

King of Zululand after his brother was dethroned.

On the 20th of April, at Kambula, we found the sun's meridian altitude to be 50° 58' 30" latitude 27° 32' 12" but on the 21st found the latitude to be 27° 37'.

On the 22nd we left General Wood's column to join our commandant at Balte Spruit, our regiment, or corps, being allowed time to get into some shape now the various detachments were finally joined. Our strength was then some 260 men and 240 horses.

On the 23rd the men were edified by the sight of a punishment parade, two regulars were flogged; this gave them food for most wholesome reflection.

On the 29th we went wood-cutting, with a party of the 80th, to Dornberg, some twelve miles from Balte Spruit; the Dornberg Hill was full of game, deer and guinea-fowl, with a few hares; on our return we shot a splendid water-buck.

At Balte Spruit we were kept constantly on the alert, with incessant patrols, the officer commanding the station being fearfully vigilant. He had one special bugbear in an inoffensive-looking knoll called Bambas Kop, some seven miles off; this seemed to require looking to at all hours of the day; during the three weeks we were at Bambas Kop, the most vigilant search failed to discover anything larger than an ant on it at any time.

On the 30th of April we had a small skirmish with some forty Zulus. Our party consisted of myself and white orderly with seven Basutos. We were reconnoitring some six miles over the Zulu border, and were suddenly fired on; the Basutos loosed off in all directions wildly, they were so excited. The scene was characteristic, the Zulus shouting challenges to the Basutos to come up the hill, the Basutos challenging the Zulus to come down; both parties fired at random, and the only damage done was a broken rifle-stock, which a huge bullet from an elephant-gun had shivered. The Basutos used to level their guns over their horses' heads with one hand and fire wildly; they are nevertheless capital Irregulars, the best scouts in the world, hardy, active, and enduring, their only faults are their excitability and their random shooting. Colonel Redvers Buller coming up an hour later saw the Zulus, but they retreated along the rocky range of hills; a large magazine of grain was burnt.

The scenery in this part of Zululand is much the same as in Natal, the same rolling *plateaux* broken by hills, rugged and stony, with table-tops; no trees are to be seen except just under the summit of a hill,

41

the sort of tree is called by the soldiers cabbage-tree wood, the leaf is like a cabbage-leaf, and the wood like that of an elder-tree; it is wet and full of pith.

When we could get leave, which was but seldom, the banks of the Blood River were searched for game, and we got duck, snipe, partridge, quail, and Cape pheasant; tolerably thickly on the plains were *pauw*, a bird as large as a turkey, and very good eating. Dornberg gave pea-fowl, guinea-fowl and hare. The Blood River was full of fish, *barbel*, or something like them, I believe the real name is *siluroid*. Once we got a bigger fish in the Blood River, to wit, a man who had been drowned while crossing on horseback in a flood; he had some £200 in gold and notes in his pockets, which he had won at cards from his comrades; he was buried on the bank then and there.

On the 5th of May we first saw the Prince Imperial, a day or two later we were on a three days' patrol with him; the force was 300 strong, under Colonel Buller, and was one of the usual patrols which he so often made, indeed, no sooner was he back from one patrol of three days, than he was off on another of the same length. At Balte Spruit the prince asked for the Frenchmen of the regiment, with these he shook hands and chatted, giving them sovereigns; two of the men taking a matter-of-fact view of the business, came and offered a sovereign for a bottle of brandy. We gave them two other sovereigns in exchange for their two; I am sorry to say we gave them some brandy also, though I believe we laid ourselves open to a severe punishment; we little thought at the time how soon we should prize these as relics.

The prince's passion for information was boundless, and the questions he used to put searching in the extreme. For instance, he would ask, "How many biscuits in a bag?" of course, the unhappy commissariat officer thus tackled broke down; the next question would be, "How many in a barrel?" then: "Are there more in a barrel than a bag?" to all the answer would be the same; the prince would then remark, "Great want of organization," and down would go the whole thing in his note-book. Then perhaps he might begin to query about the different qualities of the grass around him, and soon knew the difference between sweet and sour *veldt*, what animals would do best on the former and what on the latter.

We again joined the column at Wolff's Hill, and got our first coal fatigues, the manner of mining would make a Northumberland miner stare in surprise. The coal lay in a regular *strata* through a hill, the cutting was just made like a quarry; the men who used to get it were mostly Cornish miners of the 13th and 90th Regiments; as extra pay they got one shilling additional *per diem*, but as the damage done to their clothes was considerable, I don't think they profited much.

Meridian altitude on the 9th of May was 44° 54', and latitude was 27° 46'. Wolff's Hill lay on the south side of the Umvelosi River, some three miles off, and was some eight miles off Kambula on the northern bank.

On the 12th of May the corps got sixty new horses from the Remount Committee, which made up the strength to the full number. Our adjutant, Captain Whalley, left us here, to our great regret, to take command of a separate corps. On the 14th of May another patrol came off, but no considerable body of the enemy were seen, the chief good done was the survey of the existing road or track to Ulundi, and the discovery of another new one. On the 15th of May the Headquarters of the corps left Belte Spruit for Wolff's Hill, halting one night on the banks of the Blood River, where the 94th were stationed, with some artillery, Bettington's Horse and Native Horse, the whole in *laager*— Colonel Davies, of the Grenadier Guards, in command. On the 18th another three days' patrol went to verify previous observations made as to the route. The men left were employed in guards, fatigues, escorts and coal-cutting. About this time the bodies of Lieutenant Williams, 58th, and Lieutenant Potter were buried, they were among the slain at Zlobane, the patrol was commanded by General Wood himself, and the bodies were found under the Zunguin neck.

Lord William Beresford, 9th Lancers, joined here as staff officer to Colonel Buller; he had got six months leave from India, which he was using in Africa, he had been at the capture of Ali Musjid in Afghanistan. The duties of a staff officer must have been very heavy here, having to deal with the rough men of the Irregular Horse, and to take the records of adjutants more or less incompetent and unfit for their work; however, the duties of staff officer were done well enough, even to please a man like the colonel, who required all things done thoroughly well. In all things Colonel Buller was the same, and nothing better describes him than "Thorough". The *Kaffirs* and Zulus called him the "Steam Engine," or rather their equivalent for it. This was from his ubiquity, and, indeed, he was truly ubiquitous.

One morning in the gray mist stealing up some mountain side at the break of day, bursting suddenly on cattle *kraals*, and capturing and carrying off their inmates in face of a force more numerous by far than his own little band. Another time he would do some dashing act, like the burning of the Magulosine military *kraal*, an exploit hardly heard of at home; with a small force of 120 men the colonel burnt a large *kraal* in face of an enemy seven times as numerous, to add to the difficulty it was situated in extremely rugged ground; his opponents were a regular drilled regiment, but he brought off his force without any loss of life. He was stern and unbending to all around him, but no one could help both liking and admiring one who practised what he preached. He never flinched from hard work, and looked ever after the safety of the column with his scouts. It was a sight to see him standing on some eminence, such as an ant-heap, in the hottest fire, calmly looking through his telescope; cool and self-reliant, he always waited for his chance, when it came, no one took advantage of it quicker or used it with such effect.

The day's duties were as follows as a rule. The camp reveille sounded at five a.m., every one turned out, and fell in with carbines, the roll was called, they then stood to arms till disperse sounded. Then came stables and feeding; the grain ration per horse was five pounds weight, given in two feeds of two and a half pounds each at six a.m. and five p.m.; when more grain could be got a feed was given at eight p.m., most men could make up that feed from the grain foraged. The men then dispersed for breakfast, after which the horses were let out under the guard. At ten a.m. the defaulters and prisoners came up for punishment, which were either fines or extra guards. At eleven a.m. came drill or carbine inspection. At twelve dinner came. The various fatigues had then to be got through. At five the horses came in and were groomed and fed, at a quarter to six an alarm bugle went and the men got into their places, and so accustomed were they to this that in the darkest night they knew their appointed place.

In the meantime the adjutant had got the next day's orders from the staff officer who had received them at Headquarters' tent, submitted them to Colonel Buller and by him been distributed. The mounted corps orders were then read with the regimental to the men. These orders went through three stages, and were first Headquarters orders, then Mounted Corps orders and lastly Regimental orders. They went through many various hands before being read, but the whole process only took an hour. The Regimental orders told off corps or troops, the duties for next day, and position of troops.

The duties on the marching days were various, reveille went at quarter past four as a rule, breakfast (after feeding horses) at five, tents, kits, and stores on waggons and march at quarter past six. Two hours of hard work for all hands. One troop might be in advance of column, another reserve, a third rearguard. The post most coveted was the advance guard, which moved off at five a.m., scouting the country round; if anything was seen, intelligence was at once sent to the general commanding column and to Colonel Buller.

It was seldom, however, that the colonel was anywhere but in advance, for even after the column had got to its resting place, which it usually did at three p.m.. Colonel Buller would go with a small patrol and search a radius of seven miles round the camp, not returning till seven at night often. Only one meal a day could be taken, dinner in the evening, breakfast used to be snatched while moving about in the morning in some sort of way. The food was always the same, the same eternal beefsteak, tough as a boot-sole; how our poor teeth suffered. We never realized the old Eton epithet of "tugmutton" before we took a piece of trek ox between our jaws which recoiled from the shock. Our cooks had no inventive powers, so it was beefsteak ever and ever, even putting it through a sausage machine did not soften it one whit, the only result was the flinty pieces chipped off were smaller in dimension. The vegetables were sometimes given out in the shape of "compressed vegetable," but the men often used these instead of tobacco, smoking them.

For ourselves, though the great tobacco question came often home to us, we never were so utterly reduced as this. The tobacco of the country made by the Boers, and called Boer tobacco, is vile at first, but one gets really to like it after a time. A piece of Zulu tobacco picked up in a kraal, tided us over the worst; it was as all the Zulu tobacco is, of excellent flavour and quality, though rather dry. The Zulus themselves use it for snuff, smoking a plant called *Docker*, resembling our wild carrot, it is of a strong and pungent flavour and rapidly stupefies the user; their pipes are made of a cow's horn with a reed stem, they are fond of blowing the smoke through the water, this they do by means of another reed. They sneeze and the eyes water violently as they suck in the strong smoke. They also pound the tobacco and make snuff; when taking snuff they sit down invariably and take huge pinches solemnly.

The tea and coffee served out to the men was most excellent in quality and abundant in quantity, sugar very fair: we soon learnt to take our tea without milk.

The worst of the meat was, it had been only an hour or two killed before served out to the men; the result was dysentery. The man who invented any mode of making beef tender deserved a medal. One thing we always got was bread, to this we. are indebted to Sir Evelyn Wood, who always made arrangements for the bakery himself, and insisted on its being continually at work. He used to make arrangements for its transit himself, and the moment we reached camp it was at work; it was going all night, and till the last moment before the start.

On the 24th May, the Queen's birthday, a ration of rum was served to the men, (the soldiers called it *Dabulamanzi*—"twice watered"), it was Natal rum, however, and much diluted. On the 25th May, we left Wolff's Hill on our forward march; on the way we had an alarm to see how long the waggons would be getting packed into *laager*. It was, as a trial, a complete success, two laagers were formed in an incredibly short time, the Irregulars scoured the country round, infantry skirmishers were advanced, and all things done as if a real attack was intended.

We camped at Mundhla Hill, the advance saw a few Zulus. A new draft of horses from the Remount Committee here reached us, and some of our used up ones left for the Government Farm to recruit. On the 31st May one man was lost through his own carelessness, he was on cattle guard, and left his post to get wood and was never seen again.

On the first of June, our column moved forward to join Newdigate, like ourselves, converging on the Itylezi River. Newdigate's column had been collected at Conference Hill and Dornberg. It consisted of the 17th Lancers, the 1st Dragoon Guards, the 21st Royal Scots Fusiliers, 24th (1st and 2nd battalions), the 58th and the 94th Regiments. Only two of the regiments, the 1st and 2-24th, were the first invaders of the Zulu territory, all the others were reinforcements. Besides the regulars were Bettington's Horse and Shepstone's Basutos, with some Native Irregulars. The Imperial cavalry filled the Colonists with wonder, the size of the horses and equipments of the men, being the two chief attractions. The question here asked most frequently was, would the English horses stand the same amount of work as our handy little beasts on the same amount of grain. The regiments looked but poorly by our column, the majority of the troops were but boys; our two regiments were bearded men, the 13th, who had been in the Transvaal since the Annexation, and who had been through Secocoeni's war in particular. The 90th Light Infantry had also taken part in the old Colony war, and was a comparatively old regiment.

Of course, it took, as ever, some time for officers and men to get used to the country, and the freaks were absurd in some cases.

An officer of the —— regiment, on arrival at the Buffalo River, at once jumped to the conclusion that there were herds of buffalo round. He immediately asked his colonel for leave, and went out with an express to stalk; he was much disappointed to find but one buffalo, which, after a patient stalk, he shot. It needed the chaff of his comrades, and the assurances of the conductor to make him realize that he had shot a sick trek ox. The huge horns of the Cape ox look quite different to ordinary cattle, and gave some colour to the mistake. The narration of facts that came under the observation of the writer, with reference to the death of the Prince Imperial, will follow.

CHAPTER 6

The Prince Imperial

When, at the end of March, 1879, the telegram flashed from Cape Town, announced to the people of Natal that Prince Louis Napoleon had arrived in one of the transports, the *Danube*, great was the excitement felt. Intelligence had been received at Cape Town of his coming only a short time before his ship arrived, and Lady Frere at Government House had made every preparation for his reception. But his stay was a short and hurried one, for he arrived late one day and left the next. Lady Frere received him on the footing of a distinguished foreigner travelling, and at once sent out invitations for a reception at Government House, which took place on the same evening.

The prince arrived at Durban on the 31st of March, that is two days after Kambula had been fought. His voyage out had been a pleasant and merry one. On board, besides himself, there were many other "unattached "people who were coming out to seek for glory and excitement in the Zulu war. There were militia men, retired army men, and one or two staff officers who had been permitted to come out and find employment.

These men, who were then and afterwards chaffingly known by the name of "*desperadoes*," were so numerous that one day on board they formed themselves into a regular parade, the prince inspecting them, and very amusing, was the muster, the most mild-and-obese-looking appearing in the most warlike dress and hung round with the most bloodthirsty weapons.

The Prince Imperial was met at Durban by some staff officers then at the base. As far as the work inseparable to those busy times at the base of operations permitted, every attention was shown him by the officers in command there. The day after his arrival a mounted orderly was placed at his disposal by Major Huskisson, commandant at the base, accompanied by whom, he rode about the town and visited the different offices.

Lord Chelmsford himself was then advancing to the relief of Ekowe, and Colonel Bellairs, D.A.G., was the senior officer at Durban.

The prince became the guest of Captain and Mrs. Baynton. Captain Baynton is the agent of the "Union Line." This most kind couple, whose hospitality to every officer resident at Durban was unbounded, occupied Government House, a large residence, and there the Prince was made, and felt quite at home during his stay at Durban.

He was first attached to Major Le Grice's battery of artillery, which was encamped at Cato's Manor, some two or three miles from the town. There they made themselves very comfortable, one of the large Indian tents which had been sent from Ceylon with the 57th Regiment, making a capital officers' mess tent. The prince himself was still often seen at Mrs. Baynton's, and at the Natal club.

A personal acquaintance with him only increased the interest which naturally attached to his peculiar position. He was a most bright and engaging gentleman, and full of life and vitality. He not only took a keen interest in the Zulu war, but conversed upon and criticized our movements with much quickness, combined with judgement. There was a great freshness and *gaieté de coeur* about him, and even in some remarks he evinced a boyishness, not perhaps often found now-a-days in one of his age. He showed no great content with his position in the artillery, remarking in conversation that the artillery was from its very nature unsatisfactory to serve with, as it gave no opportunity for a close personal contact with the enemy.

Certainly to achieve personal distinction was the great object he had placed before himself. When at Durban he received a most courteous message of welcome from His Excellency Sir Bartle Frere, who was then in the Transvaal.

On the 9th of April, Lord Chelmsford arrived from Ekowe, after his victory at Gingelhovo. The day after he gave the Prince Imperial a position as extra A.D.C. on his staff. The delight of Prince Louis on receiving it was immense. Whilst at Durban the prince suffered a good deal from the fever of the place, and thus again had to take refuge in the house of Mrs. Baynton, where indeed he left his *major-domo* when he finally departed for the front to join the headquarter staff. At Durban one of his horses died. At Pietermaritzburg he was again laid up. He left the place towards the end of April and proceeded up country, stopping one night at Ladysmith, where he was entertained by the resident magistrate, Mr. Moodie.[1]

It appears that when he reached the headquarter staff, he became tired of the rather inactive life that an extra A.D.C. would have to lead while headquarters were halting in camp, and that, therefore, yielding to his urgent wishes, Lord Chelmsford attached him to the department of the quartermaster-general. Here those opportunities of a closer acquaintance with the enemy were eagerly seized on and much appreciated by him. He was ever foremost in the forays and reconnaissances in which, to his delight, he was able to take part; and it began to be felt, that, unless he was more cautious, his life would certainly be at some time or other very much endangered, beyond even the ordinary risks attending such a warfare.

One day when out on a reconnaissance with Captain Bettington (a brave and experienced officer) they were fired on from a *kraal* At once drawing his sword the Prince dashed forward, crying "Come along Bettington, come along Bettington," and it was all that officer could do to repress his inexperienced ardour. On another occasion, when on a three days' patrol with Colonel Buller and the mounted corps of the flying column, some Zulus were seen on the top of a hill. The advance was ordered to feel their strength, the prince was dashing forward and trying to head the charge when he was at once recalled and kept in check by the officer in command of the advance, thus going with, instead of before, as he had intended. The Zulus had, however, decamped before they could be got at, the ground was too rough for pursuit, and but a few shots were sent after them.

These two instances serve to show how eager and even rash he became in the presence of the enemy. The news of the death of the prince fell like a thunderbolt on all; at first it was regarded as one of those reports that so often went the rounds. Bit by bit, however, it assumed a form: first, one heard how Colonel Wood and Buller with their escort had met the flying party, then the particulars were heard as to the strength of the party with the Prince, and lastly the number of killed leaked out. Even then people were incredulous, only half believing the dreadful tale. The two questions first asked were, what will they say at home? and secondly—the poor empress.

All was the wildest excitement, brave men absolutely broke down under the blow. To them it looked a black and bitter disgrace. The

1. The prince at Ladysmith stayed at the Royal Hotel. The landlord was so charmed with his generosity that he declared his intention of naming his house "The Prince Imperial."

chivalrous young prince repaying the hospitality shown him by England, with his sword—entrusted to us by a widowed mother—to have been killed on a mere paltry reconnaissance—to have fallen without all his escort being first killed!—to lie there dead and—alone! Many there were who would have given up life to have been lying dead with him, so that our English honour might have been kept sacred. This was not to be, however; destiny, a power which has made itself so mysteriously felt in the history of his House had willed it otherwise.

Still the fact was borne in mind that none had seen the body, that none had seen a deathblow struck, so there might be hope, however great were the grounds for despair. Those who knew the proud high spirit of the prince, knew what must have occurred; they felt that, no matter what were the odds against him, he would go down with his face to the foe, and selling his life dearly.

There was little sleep in camp that night, and long after "lights out" went, men were grouped together talking of the disaster. It was said how in after years, when the whole of the Zulu War would be written in a line of history, when to all but the student it would be a forgotten episode, this would still be remembered. Then it was said how foreigners could taunt us on our care of the young knight who had put himself into our hands. All that night the body of the dead prince lay alone under the dew and frost of an African moon. In the earliest daylight the strong advance guard went out to seek for the remains. A long ride over rough ground, brought us to a sort of pass in the rocky range of small hills that lay around a large plain. Keeping along the slope of these we rode on, having all the time the *kraal* in sight where the tragedy had been enacted.

At last we came to it:—where from the rugged tops of the small hills the land sweeps gently down to the Itylezi River, the *kraal* stands; it is of moderate size, and with the usual stone wall encircling the cattle enclosure which is in its midst. It is surrounded on all sides by mealie fields, and with between these there grows the long coarse grass of the country, some three or four feet in height. The *kraals* are cut off on the southern side by these same rugged hills, on the east by the Itylezi River, lying some few hundred yards off. It is a treacherous river, full of quicksands. On the north, at a distance of three hundred yards, there is a deep gorge, or "*donga*," whilst on the west there are some smaller dongas. In fact, the whole place was like a trap. Once across the deep *donga* there is a good galloping ground, with short grass, where mounted men would run no danger of being surrounded.

51

The prince with his party seem, after having arrived at this *kraal*, at once to have off-saddled, and proceeded to the work of sketching the country to be travelled over, and verifying their previous observations. Their horses were turned out into the mealie fields without a guard; the party knew they would not stray while they had plenty of food so close at hand. The wonder is the Zulus did not drive off the horses and then attack the riders. They probably knew that the disparity of numbers was not great enough to admit of their attacking without the advantage of a surprise.

No *vedettes* seem to have been posted, nor a single precaution taken to avoid a surprise; even when the native who was with the party told them he saw a Zulu in the valley and coming towards them, no special alteration seems to have taken place in their arrangements.

The party consisted, besides the prince, of six white Colonial troopers, one infantry officer, and a friendly native. The prince had brought his dog with him, and there were also a couple of spare horses.

The observations having been made and lunch finished, nothing remained but to saddle up and get homewards. The order to bring in the horses was given, and they were then saddled and bridled. The orders were given: "Stand to your horses"; "Prepare to· mount"; and just as the final order "Mount" came, there flashes all round from the mealie gardens the hurried volley. None were hit, but all were taken by surprise, and the harm was done. Then came the swift rush with furious and demoniacal yells: no time was there to unsling carbines and mount and load. The enemy were, in one rush, upon them.

All self-control was lost; it was a general stampede. When one horse broke away, the others were impatient to follow. The prince's horse, most probably fretting at the movement of the others, moved after them, the prince vainly endeavouring to mount. It is more than probable that he was half carried, half ran by his horse for some hundred yards towards the deep *donga* on the north, when the increased strain broke the holster-straps that goes over the pommel of the saddle. His last hold on life broke with that piece of worthless leather. In the meantime, one of the men, hampered with a spare horse, and his own falling under him, had been killed at once, and his body lay not five yards from that of his horse.

The other, Trooper Abel, was most probably also unable to get on his horse, and was killed in the same *donga* as was the prince. Ere the prince lost hold of his horse, a trooper, a Frenchman, La Touche by name, dashed by him. La Touche had mounted at the volley, and in hurriedly doing so had dropped his carbine, and thus nearly lost his life. For he jumped off and regained it, and his horse moved on ere he could remount.

La Touche, however, managed to fling himself on, and with the reins in one hand and the carbine in the other, and lying on his breast on the saddle, was carried past the prince, to whom, in passing, he cried in French, "Haste, sir, there is no time to lose!" The prince, his horse having broken from him, now appears to have run towards the *donga* on the north, probably with the hope that some of them might pick him up behind them, or rally on the other side of the *donga*; having broken through the circle of enemies he may have thought that his own party could catch his horse and he would be enabled to mount on the other side. There is but little doubt that could a stand have been made on the other side, a few carbine shots might have arrested the pursuit. All were too scattered for that however. To the edge of this *donga* he reached, when finding that escape was impossible and rescue hopeless, and disdaining to fly further, he seems to have turned on the end of a spit of land which ran into the deep *donga*, and was protected on either side by smaller *dongas* running into the large one.

It is more than probable that his pursuers were close after him, though some may have been engaged with the two men who were killed between him and the *kraal*. Here he may have made a stand for a moment or two, till pierced with an *assegai*, either thrust or thrown, he staggered back into the smaller *donga* on his right, in which his body was found. Then his destroyers jumping down after him, pierced him with those eighteen *assegai* wounds which were found on him. The stab through the right eye must have caused instantaneous death; most of the others were flesh wounds only. The native who was with them broke through the circle of foes, but was overtaken and killed some distance off by his swift pursuers.

The broken relics of the party continued their course till they reached Colonels Wood and Buller, who were out some little distance in front of the Flying Column. The results of search for the fallen were as follows:—On arriving at the *kraal* after skirmishing through the long grass and mealie fields, the first body found was that of Trooper Abel, who lay dead, riddled with *assegai* wounds, and with the usual Zulu *coup de grace*[2] given with more than ordinary vigour; some yards to his front lay his horse, not yet dead, though unable to rise or do

---

2. This mark, inflicted on the bodies of the slain, consists of a gash in the stomach. It is given, it is believed, from superstitious motives.

more than move his head and forequarters, thus the incarnate fiends had left him in his agony, the earth all torn with his ineffectual struggles to rise.

To the left of this was the body of Rogers, the other trooper; it was in a *donga*, and grim was its aspect as it stood propped up against a bank, glaring into space with open eyes that had a ghastly horror in them; he too was pierced with wounds and had received the *coup de grace*.

Amongst those who were taking part in the search, was Lieutenant Dundonald Cochrane, of the 32nd Regiment (then in command of the Basutos). He it was who first discovered the body. We, riding down the edge of the same *donga*, saw Lieutenant Cochrane on exactly the opposite side, and noticed him stop suddenly and then reverently take off his hat. The body lay between us. Looking down we knew that all our vague hopes were gone, for in the *donga* below lay the last remains of him who but one day before had been so full of life and brightness. The body was naked, save that a small chain with some charms hung round the neck, and one stocking was on the right foot. The aspect was that of the very gentlest repose, and the face was smiling and peaceful as in sleep. Something of dignity in the look of the dead body must have shown the Zulus, ferocious and uncivilised though they be, that no common foe had been struck down by them. The dress was the same they had seen on other officers, too many of whom had fallen by their *assegais*, yet it was evident they recognised something of superiority in his aspect, for the *coup de grace* was inflicted by the lightest hand.

But why go on with a narrative that only raises the perpetual thought—might he have been rescued?

A few yards from him lay the body of his little white terrier, who at least was faithful, and stayed till an *assegai* laid him dead by his master's side.

Soon there came down to the spot a sad group, and all in reverence stood round the body of the dead prince. General Marshall, Mr. Forbes, the correspondent, and many officers were grouped together.

The correspondent of the French *Figaro*, with the unrestrained passion of his nation, threw himself down by the body, weeping and wringing his hands in uncontrollable grief. The body was placed by officers in a blanket, and deposited in an ambulance which had now arrived, and taken to the camp of the second column, into which it was followed by the general and all the officers.

Nothing further was discovered on close examination round the spot where the prince had fallen. Whether he used his revolver will probably never be known; most likely he used his sword which he loved so well. It had been his father's. As far as we could tell at the time, the Zulus who killed the prince were a small party to whom the *kraal* belonged, and who were gathering mealies in the neighbouring fields when the party got to it. The prince's shirt was found the next day in the possession of a Zulu woman. She, poor, old, and blind, manifested the greatest indifference to the questions which were eagerly put to her.

The body of the prince was conveyed from the headquarter camp in an ambulance. On arriving near Ladysmith, it remained at the beginning of the village, upon the *veldt*, during the night, a guard furnished by the garrison being mounted over it. Here took place perhaps the most touching, because the most simple, scene in the whole of the long progress to the last resting place at Chiselhurst. From a schoolhouse near had come out and formed on each side of the road a line of black school children. Their harmonium had also been carried out; as the rough ambulance drew near they commenced singing an hymn. There was much of pathos in the sound of the sweet sad strain uprising in the chill morning air; this entirely spontaneous mark of sympathy for the "young chief" was but one proof of the feeling that all in the colony, whatever their age, colour, position or sex, had at the sudden and terrible close of that bright young life.

And it may be safely affirmed that not one dissociated in his mind, from the thought of the dead son, the recollection of the blow awaiting the widowed mother. In Ladysmith itself, the body was met by a detachment of the 58th Regiment under Captain Churchill, and some Colonial forces.[3] Lieutenant Alan Hill, 58th, and an escort from that regiment escorted it down to Pietermaritzburg. At Durban the population for thirty miles round attended to witness the procession; six hundred British soldiers under Major (now Lieutenant-Colonel) Huskisson were under arms. The most striking scene was at the point where the military handed over the coffin to the Royal Navy. Captain Bradshaw of H.M.S. *Shah*, and Commodore Richards had all the blue jackets drawn up there. Lieutenant-Colonel Pemberton, 60th Rifles preceded him in military charge of the body on board H.M.S. *Orontes*.

---

3. These forces consisted of the Ladysmith Town Guard under Captain Randalls, and fifty armed natives under the Resident Magistrate.

The poor *major-domo* who was, as before mentioned, left behind in Durban, was inconsolable at the death of his young master I indeed it was feared that even his reason would be affected by the shock. He frequently repeated what everyone who had known the chivalrous young prince must have felt to be the simplest truth, "My master would never have abandoned one of them." We feel we have strayed from the direct course of our narrative in giving these details, but so little has been published about the life of the Prince Imperial in South Africa that we are sure this digression will be pardoned.

On the night succeeding the discovery of the prince's body, while we were encamped on the Itylezi River, one man was wounded in the shoulder with an *assegai*—some Zulu on the opposite bank had thrown it at him while he was filling his canteen.

CHAPTER 7

A Brisk Skirmish

On the 4th of June, while on patrol with Colonel Buller, about 2500 Zulus tried to entrap us, but they were discovered in time, and their attempt failed. On receipt of this intelligence in camp all the horse were ordered out, and the laager surrounded with an earthwork. This force of the enemy was thought to be the advance guard of a larger body. The next day at dawn most of the Irregular Horse of the Flying Column were sent out under Colonel Buller to reconnoitre in advance. A body of lancers and dragoons from General Newdigate's column following some little time later.

On reaching the place where the ambuscade was laid the day previous, a dark mass of Zulus were seen in the plain below. They were gathered round some large *kraals*, which proved to be those of Sirayo.

It was a lovely scene we looked down on from the rocky hill where we stood. The morning sun had just risen over the hill opposite us, and shone on the river that ran at its base. Between the river and the hill was a small open plain. The *kraals* stood in the centre of the plain. The sides of the hill was seamed and torn with dongas, and clothed with mimosa bush. There were some among us who had not seen trees for two months. Far on the left front rose Inhlazatye, gleaming in the morning sun, the great greenstone mountain beyond which the king's place, our goal, lay. On the right rose Ibabanango, which we were soon to cross. A swarm of Zulus were flitting like bees round the huts below, and we could see some waggons, spoil of Isandula, close to the *kraal*.

We had plenty of time to see this as we rode down the gentle slope to the river.

With Colonel Buller one is not kept long in suspense; the orders were soon given, "Frontier Light Horse the centre, Baker's Horse the left, and Whalley's the right". The Zulus, in the meantime, had massed and moved off in companies, and taken up a position in the *dongas* at the foot of the hill. They were sheltered also by the thick cover afforded by the bush and grass. Once across the river, we advanced at a gallop, firing the *kraal*, the enemy opening fire at once. We rode to within three hundred yards of them; the men dismounted, and the horses were led some few yards out of the hottest of the fire.

The men took cover in the long grass and behind ant-heaps. They fired fairly steadily, but the hill side was covered with aloes, which looked like men among the smoke, and which were often doubtless hit. Colonel Buller was standing on an ant-heap looking through his glass, watching the effects of the fire. This continued some time, till the enemy, trying to outflank us on the right, poured in a volley at some eighty yards from the edge of a mealie field to which they had crept. The order was then given to retire, which was done in good order, and the river was recrossed and the men drawn up on the other side. A war correspondent, who had been lying under an ant-heap and firing away, did not hear the order to retire given, so he was left behind, till the colonel told someone to go back and put him on his horse. From an accident to his leg he was unable to mount, but he was brought off all safely.

Apart from the chance of getting hit, the scene was pretty in the extreme, to see the whole face of the hill dotted with little puffs of white smoke. We had eight or ten men hit, none mortally, and some fifteen horses killed or wounded. The Imperial cavalry had meanwhile come on the scene, and by General Marshall's order advanced to the attack. It was a grand sight, to do one's heart good, to see them advancing across the level plain. They crossed the river and then moved forward over the little plain, the Lancers in advance and the King's Dragoon Guards in support. They took up nearly the same ground as that which we had previously occupied. One could not help being sorry they were sent there; it was a mere waste of life. The enemy were too strongly posted to have any serious damage done to them.

It was hopeless to expect cavalry to turn them out, and the result must inevitably be a retreat. The main object had already been gained, the enemy having shown their strength. The result was the cavalry had to retreat after losing one of their best officers, Lieutenant Frith, their adjutant; they also had a horse or two hit, I believe. They then retired and drew up out of sight of the Zulus, behind a gentle rise. By this concealment the Zulus were to be induced to move out into the plain.

The cavalry leaders had however yet to find that Zulus were not to be duped by so transparent a ruse, and the sight of half the lances with the fluttering pennons which stuck up over the brow of the hill too plainly marked the position of the (otherwise) wily lancers. Of course, by all the rules of war, the Zulus should have been drawn out and then cut up, but they are very old-fashioned. Some few crept down the rugged bed of the river and fixed scattered shot at us. We, the Irregulars, in the meantime,, sat and lounged about, the bait of the trap, but they were too wary. To the voice of the charmer, English cavalry general though he was, they would not listen.

Soon the order was given to return home, which was some couple or three miles off, the column having advanced a few miles since we left.

In the Itylezi River close to where the body of the prince had been discovered, gold was panned out by a trooper, an old Californian miner, whether in paying quantities we cannot say. We believe it is seldom in South African gold digging that gold can be got in river beds. Specimens of quartz sent down to be analysed to a first-rate engineer in the colony, showed indications, and paying ones, of gold. The whole country round this district is without doubt auriferous. The question is how much return for labour.

On the 6th or 7th of June we were roused some half hour or so after "lights out" by the sound of big guns from General Newdigate's column. This column was encamped some few miles to the rear of ours, at a place known afterwards as "Fort Funk". An officer was sent over and came back with accounts of the scare. It appears an alarm took place, the men hurried to their stations in the *laager*, leaving their tents standing. Then one fired, now another, and at last the firing ran all down the line utterly beyond the power of the officers to stop. The big guns joined in and increased the tumult. The firing gradually died out all down the line. The next business was to inspect the damage. The sight was *not* particularly edifying, tents riddled, clothes in a similar condition, oxen shot, and their drivers frightened to death.

We were much rejoiced to find that the only troops who had not shared in the panic were those under Major Chard, V.C., a portion of our column, who had gone to assist in making a fort in front of the laager. The fort was luckily far enough advanced in building to afford shelter against the fire of the *laager*, not only for the engineers, but also for the picket who fortunately took refuge there. The stones in the fort embankment showed abundant traces of the fire, most of the stones were marked by bullets, one had received four hits. A sergeant was shot on the spot, and only lived a few days. I do not know if any other casualties occurred.

It was then decided by Lord Chelmsford that Wood's column should go back to their base—Utrecht—and bring in all the supplies from that place. Most of the mounted troops with Colonel Buller joined General Newdigate's column. This was the 7th June. The same night the laager was formed close to where the skirmish of the 5th took place. A few shots of the big guns were fired at some of the enemy who were hanging about the *kraals*. The waggons that were by the *kraals* were also discovered and used. On the next morning some infantry skirmished through the bush but did not see any trace of the enemy.

One of our officers had a servant, an old Colony black, who went by the name of Ketchwayo, who, on our arrival in camp, bolted off, as they always did, to get wood. While engaged in pulling a *kraal* to pieces, some regulars who were being sent out as cattle guards saw him, they immediately gave chase to him and collared him. The poor fellow was most fearfully frightened, and when asked his name could only gasp out "Ketchwayo." "Oh, you are the very fellow we want," and so poor Ketchwayo was marched off in high triumph. The men were fearfully sold when the truth came out that he was only Captain D'Arcy's servant and not the King of the Zulus.

We found the arrangements of Newdigate's column were not nearly so perfect as those of our own column, and most ardently we looked for its return. Every day some story about peace went the rounds of the camp; ambassadors of more or less dubious respectability kept coming in. All this we heard with a sore heart, for a great longing to avenge the death of the poor prince was in us. All would have thought it a disgrace had not an opportunity to wipe out that terrible stain on our escutcheon been vouchsafed us.

Colonel Buller still continued to carry on his patrols, and we were employed mending drifts to facilitate the return of Wood's column.

On the 13th June, the Zulus were reported to be in force some few miles off, which proved a false report, for a patrol sent out to look them up could discover nothing. On this patrol we saw a completely new hut built where some had been burnt a few days previously.

A small patrol under the colonel exchanged shots about this time with a few Zulus, and shot two of them, and had a long chase after two mounted men.

There were large maize and *Kaffir* cornfields near, which gave our horses more grain than they had had for some time. There were also small patches of *Kaffir* beans, a sort of earth nut, so on them we fared sumptuously.

On the hill behind the camp were two old Zulu women, the ugliest hags ever seen. They expressed no surprise when they saw us, but sat at the door of their huts blinking in the sun. When we brought them water and food they gave no thanks, but mumbled at the hard biscuit with their toothless jaws. Evidently their friends stole down in the night and fed them, as we found the water jugs or gourds replenished on the next day, and the old ladies were too weak to walk.

On the 14th June we left on a patrol with Colonel Buller for a mountain, some thirty-five miles off called Intabankulu, where there was a great herd of cattle reported. We travelled all day and into the night, seeing nothing, and finally encamped on the banks of Umvelosi River. The colonel always made a point of encamping in the dark, and invariably moved a few miles after sundown. The enemy then never knew where we were at night, so could not surround and attack us. The most perfect silence was always strictly enjoined. The horses were put in rings of some thirty or so each, fastened to each other, the men slept at their heads in a circle. Sentries paced round the rings all night to see that no horse broke loose.

One blanket only was carried, and the nights were most bitterly cold. The guards had to be visited hourly, and the *vedettes* also looked to. Smoking was always stopped, as the glare of the matches would have pointed out our position to the enemy. About two in the morning the men were roused, and silently loosed the horses and fell in. The saddles were never removed at night when on patrol. Then came the work of counting and whispering over the roll call. All was done in most perfect quiet. The orders, short and to the point, were given in a low tone to the men. In that rarefied atmosphere sound is heard at an incredible distance. Then comes the word to advance, and in pitchy darkness the broad river is forded, the horses slipping like cats down the steep banks, then scrambling up the equally steep banks on the further shore.

Still in silence we follow our leader through the pathless waste, to ride safely over which at a gallop in the light is no trivial matter. After six or seven miles of this sort of thing, we reach our destination; orders are given: to every troop is explained their object and duty in a terse sense or two, and then, just in the greyest dawn, we quicken to a canter, each troop diverges to its goal, and the scene, one moment before so silent, re-echoes to the hollow sounds of the hoofs of four hundred horse. The object of our present attack is a mountain, rising squarely out of a broad plain, rocky and precipitous. On the first terrace are the *kraals* of the enemy, and at this early hour their fires gleam through the darkness and are our beacons in the advance. Two troops swing round the hill in rear some climb the right, some the left face, while others dash straight on to the assigned post. The enemy, thoroughly surprised, swarm out of their *kraals*, some reach the cliffs and keep up a dropping fire on the assailants. The hill re-echoes to the sound of rifle shots as the caves among the rocks are searched one after the other. If they do not resist they are taken prisoners.

One man came to the mouth of a cave, and fired point blank at Captain and Commandant Baker; he luckily missed, and the captain promptly shot him. The shot hit the Zulu in the forehead, the distance being not six yards, yet, such is the extraordinary thickness of the skull, that the bullet flattened out on it. The enemy, in some cases, were so completely taken by surprise, that on coming to the mouth of the cave and presenting to fire, they had not taken out the little plug of newspaper that they keep in the muzzle to keep out wet. In fact, they are totally bewildered, and do not gather together in force enough to make a serious resistance. Some seven hundred cattle were captured, a herd of goats and sheep, and about forty prisoners. Many more prisoners might have been taken, but they would only have been incumbrances.

By this time the alarm had been spread all round, and the neighbouring hills had become dotted with the gathering enemy. The cattle are rapidly collected by us and driven off. The main object of the patrol—harassing the enemy—effected, we move away. The Zulus now collected, though yelling with impotent fury, dare not venture into the plain, and we march unpursued on our return journey. But look at the men driving the cattle: they are prisoners, taken just now on the hill, who by a cruel irony of fate are compelled to drive the cattle but an hour ago their own. A few women-prisoners accompany our march: it would not do to let these go as yet. They are accordingly brought on to where we halt for breakfast.

We halt near the place we encamped at the previous night. The horses, as hungry as ourselves, are let out to graze. The guards are mounted and *vedettes* posted on the rising ground. The men disperse for water and fuel, (the latter they get from the *kraals*,) others turn out the haversacks and make coffee. The provisions taken on the patrol are coffee, sugar, and biscuit, fresh beef for two days and preserved for the third. The coffee is made in "billys," like those Australian diggers have, these hang in a neat leather case by the side of the saddle. The women-prisoners are very happy indeed, though they don't know how long we shall retain them. They are only exchanging one life of slavery for another as they think, and they may have heard that Englishmen do not force their wives to work.

One good-looking damsel, with a leopard skin on her shoulders, in reply to some chaff about marriage, evinces an astuteness which we did not expect to see in a child of nature. On our humbly asking for her dusky hand, she enquires if we shall make her work in the fields? on learning that it is not our intention to make her hoe mealies, she wants to know if we are an *inkose* (chief). Another then chaffing her on the same subject, she learns that he is an *inkose inkulu* (great chief), and promptly discards her first adorer, ourselves, to our huge disgust. The captive seems, indeed, to have a great idea of her own attractions, for after this affront to us, she tries to make it up at breakfast, and gets some coffee, meat, and biscuit. Very vexed is she when she finds there is no sugar in her coffee, and she soon rectifies the omission. Some of the sheep which are hardly able to travel as far as the camp, are killed and slung on the spare horses. Some little want of discrimination as to the choice parts of the animal and the manner of eating, lowers our captive in our eyes.

The horses are now brought in and saddled up, the prisoners (female) are sent back with a message to the king. She of the leopard skin weeps piteously and begs hard to come with us: she was fully persuaded that *inkose inkulu* was going to make her his bride and carry her off. Poor girl! her rose-coloured visions are dissipated, and no doubt the old and ill-favoured hag she is with will avenge their neglect on her, especially as she gave herself rather consequential airs on the strength of her conquest. Henceforth she can look forward to nothing better than being sold as a slave to the man whom she, in company with some dozen or so fellow-slaves, have to call husband. The Zulus are a light-hearted race, and we hope she will soon recover, and live happily ever afterwards.

One thing in this war reflects credit on us all—no woman was wantonly injured, and the wildest Irregular must treat them fairly. There was an attack in *Truth* some time ago on the subject of atrocities by the Irregulars. It was not worth one's while to contradict the statement, so I suppose no one cared to, but it was utterly false.

All day we ride on, and reach camp at ten p.m., travelling the last four hours in darkness, riding down almost precipitous dongas, fording rivers, and stumbling over ant-heaps and into ant-bear holes. It would horrify a Leicestershire man to travel in the day the ground we do at night. All our cattle get safe to camp, and we soon discuss the lambs we captured in the morning.

On the 17th June we rejoin Wood's column, to our huge delight. The arrangements in the headquarter column were by no means so good as our own, spite of the abundance of staff officers. The men were harassed by being kept under arms an indefinite period in the morning. False alarms were given, and the horses did not get either the grain or the care that they did in our own column. General Wood had made his march in an incredibly short space of time; he was evidently resolved to make no unnecessary delay.

We were anxiously expecting various stores to eke out our meagre allowance, but the general would carry no unnecessary lumber, so they were left behind, and what became of them we know not.

We must be left in this uncomfortable position, till our next brings us to more stirring scenes.

CHAPTER 8

Across the Umvelosi

By this time the Irregular corps of the Flying Column had been brought to their best form. Long months of anxious work on the part of Colonel Buller and the officers under him, had resulted in the formation of a regiment the most fitted for rough work yet seen in Africa. The materials that the colonel had to work on were of all sorts. The Irregulars always reminded me of that verse, *Parthians and Medes, Elamites and Persians,* &c., comprising as they did men of all nations. My own corps included the following nationalities; English, Scotch, Irish, Welsh, French, Prussians, Danes, Swedes, Austrians, Norwegians, Italians, Spanish, Australians, Russians, Jews of all nations, Poles, Hungarians, Africanders (English born in Africa), Boers, and Americans. Surely a mixed lot to weld as they were into a perfect whole. I started, as I said before, thoroughly prejudiced against volunteers, but am bound to admit that they did good work and service.

Of these nations, Danes made the best and Americanized Irish the worst soldiers. As Archibald Forbes truly says, they were men of varied antecedents. Discharged soldiers and 'Varsity men, unfrocked clergyman and sailor, cockney and countryman, cashiered officers of army and navy here rubbed shoulders. Of course, when newly raised, these corps were for a time utterly useless. The long march up the country consolidated, and the heavy work weeded out the less strong. As everywhere the weaker went to the wall, succumbed to the climate; fever and dysentery, ague and rheumatism thinned out the weakly.

Coming from the sweltering heat of the plains to the cold frosty nights of the uplands; heated with the dusty march by the slow-moving waggons; drenched with the frequent thunder-storms, then frozen, it will not be wondered that many sank. They were, therefore, by the time they reached the column thoroughly hardened and seasoned, and as men of ruined fortunes are proverbially reckless of life, they were well suited for the work before them.

It may not be out of place to give a sketch of the various Irregular regiments.

First of all came the oldest Irregular corps,, the Frontier Light Horse, about two hundred strong. This corps was raised for the old colony war by Lieutenant, now Major Carrington, 1-12th Regiment, and was then known as Carrington's Horse; it served with distinction through the Gaika and Galeka campaigns. It bore itself always with courage, and had more *esprit de corps* than the other corps. After Carrington left it was commanded by Captain Whalley and then by Colonel Buller; under both it served through the first campaign of England against Secocoeni. It has been always well officered, and in that had a marked advantage over the other corps. It has been officered by. such men as Colonel Buller, Major Carrington (1-24th), Captain MacNaughten (killed in Perie bush), Whalley (17th Lancers), Barton (Coldstream Guards, killed at Zlobane), Prior (80th Regiment), Brunker (26th), Baron von Stitencron (Austrian Hussars, killed at Zlobane), and many others. It is now under the command of Commandant Cecil D'Arcy, V.C, who has risen to distinction and gained his V.C. in it.[1] Since disbanded.

"Baker's Horse" was originally raised by Captain now Major F. J. Baker, Ceylon Rifles, an officer who has served through the various African wars and in Borneo. It served through the latter part of the old colony war under that officer. Their adjutant at that time was Lieutenant Dalrymple, now A.D.C. to Sir Bartle Frere. After the quelling of the rebellion, and the flight of Kreli and death of Sandilli, this corps was sent to garrison Kokstadt. The Pondas were supposed to be about to rise, but were checked by the prompt measures taken. After this the regiment marched through Natal and disbanded at Port Elizabeth. A few days afterwards Captain Baker got a telegram from Lord Chelmsford to raise men. This was done with incredible celerity, and in a short space some two hundred and forty men sailed from Port Elizabeth. At Zlobane this corps suffered in common with the other Irregulars. Nevertheless, in spite of many other services during the remainder of the war, we believe Captain Baker has received no acknowledgement for his services, though his were the first reinforcements to enter Natal after Isandula.

The third force was Raafe's Rangers, and a more forbidding lot

---

1. Reported killed before Pretoria, Jan., 1881.

of mixed Hottentots and scum of the Diamond Fields was never collected together outside a prison wall.

Then came the Natal Light Horse under Captain Watt Whalley, an officer who had seen more service than falls to the lot of most men. His services include the Mutiny (wounded), China, and Abysinnia. He also served in the Papal Zouaves, and accompanied that regiment to France, serving in the Franco-Prussian War, dangerously wounded at Mézières and taken prisoner. Then through the Carlist War commanding a regiment under Don Carlos. In Africa the Gaika, Galeka (wounded), Secocoeni and Zulu campaigns. Of course, with such a commanding officer a regiment must be a good one.

The Basutos (100) were Native Irregulars, under Captain Cochrane, 32nd. This force was at Isandula, and through their knowledge of *Kaffir* warfare, they managed to extricate themselves with slight loss, though often hand to hand. As scouts they were invaluable. They were courageous, and possessed the merit of being cheap, finding their own horses and getting £3 per month. These ponies were hardy little brutes, in fact they seemed to be untirable, for let the day be ever so long at the end they were fresh. The Basutos were all Christians, many a time have we turned out and listened to them singing their hymns after reveille. Their voices are good and knowledge of time perfect.

The Mounted Infantry can hardly be called Irregulars, they were grooms, and other men picked from the various regiments. Their uniform was a red coat, more or less tattered, trousers and leggings *ditto*, with a battered helmet. They looked like a cross between a groom out of place and a soldier after a night in cells and a big drink. They have been commanded by Major Carrington, Colonel Russell, 12th Lancers, and latterly by Captain Brown, V.C, 1-24th, a most excellent officer. Their other officers were Lieutenants Davis (Buffs), Walsh, 1-13th, Hutchinson, 4th King's Own. This sort of cavalry will be the force of the future for Africa, as they are as good as any others and far cheaper.

The mounted corps of Colonel Weatheley, which was annihilated at Zlobane, were raised under Captain Denison, one of the survivors, but never again joined the Flying column.

The Kaffrarian Riflemen were the relics of the old Crimean German Legion, which was allotted lands at the Cape in 1856. They were raised under Commandant Schembrucker, one of their old officers. This corps left the column in April, and remained in the Transvaal. Some of their officers were officers now serving in the Prussian army.

Just at this time a journey to the field of Isandula was made by a large party, their report was that the site of the camp was very badly chosen. We rather expected to find the bodies lying in square, as the earlier reports of the battle had led one to suspect. The reverse, however, was the case, and this showed the ammunition had been exhausted. The terrible slaughter seems to have occurred when the retrograde move was made to the waggons. The first part of the battle had been fought some distance from the camp. The slaughter of Zulus must have been immense. Their own story shows this to have been the bloodiest battle of the war save Kambula. Long after we found many people suffering from the fearful wounds there received.

By no means the best section of the Zulu nation seem to have been there engaged. Though the King's guards, as we may say, fought, still the bold robber tribes of Umbeline, from the rocky mountain strong-holds, were not there. The regiments seem to have been drawn from the south-eastern portion of the country, from the bush region and the border land. When we consider the three battles of January 22nd and 24th—Isandula, Ineyzane, and Zlobane, we can arrive at some idea of the immense power of the Zulu nation at the commencement of the war. Pearson at Ineyzane opposes, he thinks 11,000; on the same day, 25,000 are said to overwhelm Durnsford, and retired before Lord Chelmsford; while two days later, Wood defeats 12,000 at Zlobane.

The distances between the places indicated, make it impossible that a single man could have fought at any two of these actions: Ketch-wayo had a large reserve at Ulundi, so the total fighting strength of the nation must have been some 50,000 at least. The battlefield was strewn with papers, some of them doubtless of importance, nor was it till long after that these were collected and burned. The different condition of the bodies was most remarkable, some were by the heat of the sun completely mummified, in others the ordinary process of decomposition had taken place; The fact that *vedette* duty prevented a close examination of the field, must be the apology for so poor an account of the visit.

On the 19th of June our corps' turn for advance guard fell. The two columns were this time marching nearly together, that is. General Wood's column was sometimes fire miles ahead of General Newdi-gate's, at others it would be encamped on the other side of the same river. On this morning we left camp, some hours before dawn, and thoroughly examined the ground along which the column would pass. Then breaking off into two detachments, one party turned off to examine the hills on the right of the line of march, the others, those to the left. We went to the right. After some time a few Zulus were seen leaving some *kraals*. They allowed us to get within shot, when delivering a volley, they disappeared over the crest of the hill. Long before we climb its steep sides they were out of shot.

On reaching the top, we see a large tract of prairie-like land, stretching for some distance. This *plateau* is covered with luxuriant yet sweet grass. The edges of this *plateau* fall away into deep valleys, which in their turn, are broken by rugged hills. Skirting the edge of the table-land for some time, we espy a large herd of cattle in the deep gorges, some miles below us. A number of people were driving them across a river, which twined and twisted about below. Something in their gait told our leader. Commandant Baker, that these cattle were only a bait. Orders were accordingly given not descend to capture them. Lucky it was that this was done, as the sequel shows. Some of the Zulus below were in shot. We rode to the spur of the ridge, just where it dipped down suddenly into the valley beneath, then opened fire.

No sooner had we done so, than a volley was fired from a knoll, some 200 yards off on our right. An officer was sent with some twenty-five men to dislodge them. This he did by getting on another spur that overlooked them, and thus outflanking them. Both of our little bodies now opened fire on the stragglers in the plain below, at some 600 yards. The enemy made for a *donga* a little nearer to us, we then fired into the donga at anyone showing themselves. About 300 of the Zulus were then seen to leave the further end of this ravine, and steal down the bed of the river, so that by making a detour of some two miles they could completely cut us off. Our fire was so galling to those in the *donga*, that not being able to return it effectually they bolted in large numbers from it. They then made a charge forward to dislodge us from our coign of vantage, but were repulsed, and retired leaving some thirty dead lying about the plain.

The body of the enemy, who were all this time trying to outflank us, had in the meantime crept nearly round the base of the hill, along the bed of the river which wound round it. Our commander called us off, having captured some few cows and a good flock of sheep. These we drove off, and though our friends followed us, and occasionally fired, yet they did not venture to leave the edge of the broken ground Their intention had been to lure our small force into the plain and pounce on us from their hiding place. In that case probably not a man would have escaped. This little brush is given as a type of what was constantly occurring. In the face of much superior numbers, our small force of fifty men had inflicted a loss of about forty on them. Their numbers were about 700. The party which had early in the day gone to the left, had exchanged shots with an enemy posted in an inaccessible *kloof*.

On the 21st of June we were encamped on the head waters of the Umvelosi River. Every day now more Zulus were seen, and small skirmishes took place daily. The enemy made many and determined attempts, to burn up the grass along the line of march. It required all our vigilance to prevent them doing so. The grass was dry as tinder and caught at once. Every day a broad strip was cut round the camp, so that we should not be burned out. Sometimes the enemy would burn a huge strip in our teeth, small bodies used to appear incessantly, fire a patch and then be off. Every night we lay among the black ashes.

We had been for several days in sight of what was supposed to be Ulundi. Our route lay along the top of a chain of hills, the valleys on our left full of bush. The first sight of Ulundi was glorious, the goal we had so long and ardently desired was in sight at last. That mysterious king's place of which traders had given such extravagant accounts. Truly the scene we gazed on was pleasant. For days we had travelled over rough Ibabanango through a treeless country. Here we look at from our ridge a long valley some thirty miles long, bounded by hills. The valley itself was covered with brushwood. The broad Umvelosi swept across it in the distance. Many huge *kraals* were in it each containing thousands of huts; these were the barracks to the army. Afar off was a large circular enclosure which was pointed out as the king's *kraal*. Two soldiers of the 13th testified their delight by falling out, and milling each other with right good will, in the exuberance of their delight.

At this time we passed the road where Crealock's Column were supposed to have advanced by. Long and anxiously did we scan the country in this direction. Many were the fears lest he should be before us, and snatch the laurels we thought our due. Joyful were we when no trace of him could we see. It would have made us easier if we had known that he, with his strong army corps were encamped in a marsh near a well nigh impracticable landing place.

A day or two later we descended into the valley to destroy three large military *kraals*. All expected hot work. We rode down among the bushes. On the heights above were some guns escorted by lancers. Advancing through the difficult ground, we burned without opposition the large *kraals* we found. These consisted in two cases of some 2500 huts each. The third was somewhat smaller. Many relics of Isandula were found in these barracks, baths, buckets, water canteens, cooking pots, and many other things. In one hut we found a hymn book (ancient and modern with music), in several, Roman Catholic prints of saints were seen.

Small bodies of the enemy were seen, and a partial skirmish took place, some seven of the enemy were killed. A compact column of some 2000 Zulus were seen advancing by the gunners on the hill. The guns opened fire, and the first two shells pitched right in front of them, and burst. Seeing we were so well supported, they retired. We were not sorry as the ground was bad for cavalry, and the enemy knew the ground better than we did. The hills were then climbed and we returned home. The air in these valleys was hot and fragrant, like a conservatory at home, as we got up the hills again it changed to the bracing atmosphere of the uplands. A day or two later some ambassadors from the king, bearing two huge tusks of ivory, were met and brought in. One of these tusks was huge, it took two men to carry it.

The Embassy also brought with them some 160 head of cattle, trek oxen, captured at Isandula. Their sleek and well fed appearance contrasted with our thin and travel-worn bullocks. The Embassy also expressed the king's intention to collect the cattle, captured at the upcountry fight (Intombi River), and send them to the general. The ivory was returned, and the cattle kept for some days. The ambassadors took back the answer to the king's proposals for peace. We do not know the king's proposals, but the answer was, we believe, that no proposition could, be entertained unless 1000 Zulus came in, and gave up their arms. No great diplomatic skill seems to have been exercised, and mayhap it were well there was not.

The sight of the ivory aroused the natural desire inherent in every soldier, especially inherent in those of fortune, for plunder. Vague stories of the wealth of the king went about. Splendid visions of loot, in the shape of gold dust, ivory, ostrich feathers and diamonds, filled the soldiers' eyes. Incredible stories of the amount of treasure taken at Isandula were circulated. We believe the real amount was £300. It is needless to say these golden visions were broken, not a man of the Regulars being a sovereign the better for any loot taken. Some of the Irregulars got small sums from deserted *kraals*. The amount altogether we imagine was small. The men took pains to conceal anything they did take, as they were afraid of being made to disgorge.

71

CHAPTER 9

Panic in the Camp

On the 25th we reached Magnumbonium or Introgeneni, a point 2000 feet above the sea level It is nearly at the extreme end of the chain of hills, along which we had advanced the preceding days. From it the road or tract to Ulundi branches off, and finally dips down into the lovely valley. From here a good view of the veritable Ulundi can be seen, the sight we had waited six long months for. The delight one felt must have been similar to that that animated the Ten Thousand at the first sight of the sea. One was almost tempted to shout Ulundi! Ulundi! as they did *Thalassa! Thalassa!* From the same height we could see the sea in the far distance.

The troops here got two days' rest. Then orders were given to leave all sick horses, spare waggons, tents, provisions. A fort was made, and all waggons not intended to go on left behind. They were left in charge of Major Upcher 1-24th, and 500 men. Provisions were taken for ten days.

On the morning of June 30th at 6-15, the united columns advanced and descended the slopes to the plain. The valley was thickly studded with aloes, mimosa, and other tropical trees. Some eight miles off the Umvelosi flashed and shone like a silver thread. The river that saw the fight at Kambula was to see another at Ulundi. On the descent the advanced guard was met by some messengers bearing a letter from the King, and the sword of the Prince Imperial. Ketchwayo had, at the request of Lord Chelmsford, sent for this from the hands of the small tribe by whom he had been killed.

The messengers were detained at the outpost, while the letter and sword were carried to the general. The sword, easily recognizable, by the cipher N, was gazed on with eager but respectful curiosity by all present. It was reported to have belonged to the great Napoleon, it certainly belonged to Napoleon III.

On the last occasion we had seen it, the ill-fated prince had drawn it, while galloping up a hill from the crest of which some Zulus were just decamping. He expressed an eager desire to blood it. A wish too fully fulfilled, as it most probably was in those few moments just prior to his death, when he had turned to bay. Its cold hilt was the last thing that that hand, so soon to be cold as the steel, had clasped. The letter was written by a trader named Vejn, it was addressed "From Ketchwayo to Lord Chelmsford." On the outside Vejn had, at the peril of his life, written "If you come, come strong, there are 20,000 of them."

A noble warning, this generous message, and one that ought to be remembered. There were many Zulus round the king who knew how to read English. If one of these had seen the timely warning, death and most probably torture would have been the fate of the writer of it. What anxious moments his must have been as he saw the bearers press through the crowds of Zulus round the royal *kraal*.

Continuing our route we get to the foot of the hills, and fairly into the plain. Here *laagar* is formed, and we camp for the night. Newdigate's Division some quarter of a mile from us. The water here was very bad and scarce, the journey for it long. A little generalship on the enemies' part might have seriously inconvenienced us in regard of this.

The orders of that night gave out that the irregulars of Wood's column were to leave camp at two a.m. the next morning. That hour found all ready, and we set out in the inky darkness. For several miles we pass along noiselessly. Day breaking finds us in a park-like country full of thin bush. Our ride ceases on the banks of the Umvelosi, or rather just behind the ridge that slopes down to it. Here out of sight we halt, dismount and ease our horses. The colonel rides out to survey the country. From some miles away comes the war song of the enemy, rising and falling. It is nearly impossible to describe the effect of such a mighty volume of sound, rising through the quiet air. Very weird and awesome does it seem to us, as we wait without seeing the singers. It seems they were guarding the ford below. We thought they were advancing, and every minute expected to be engaged.

Our orders were not to fire until we were fired on. We believe Lord Chelmsford had given Ketchwayo three days' grace, or until the 3rd of July, to consider his ultimation. We rode on to where the Basutos were posted on the ridge, and there looking down on the valley we see it filled completely with the enemy. They were posted at the two fords just below us. During the few moments we stayed with the Basutos, we saw two Zulu spies within one hundred yards of us. The Basutos were frantic with excitement, longing to shoot at them. It was certainly tempting, to see them creeping through the grass, it was however against orders, and Captain Cochrane would not allow it. They took a good view and then retired, soon to be succeeded by another pair. Trotting back, we see the long train of baggage-waggons descending the slopes in our rear, while ahead of them the sun flashes on the rifle barrels of the advancing column. A wide chain of *vedettes* are thrown out, completely covering the advancing regiments. The weird music still rises from the valley of the river, and much marching and counter-marching takes place among the enemy.

All of us had started without breakfast and without being able to fill our water canteens, our sufferings from thirst, as we sat under the burning sun, were something intense. Below us rolled the river, broad and cool, rippling over its shallow bed. For all the good it was to us, it might have been a hundred miles off. We could only look at it wistfully, and how savage it made us with the foe who guarded it, I think the Zulus had resolved to defend the fords, but from some un-explained reason abandoned that resolution. Soon, about 2 p.m., the advance guard reaches us. We all thought that we should be ordered to advance and take the ford. It is completely commanded by a bluff or precipice that rises immediately below it.

The idea was that Wood's column should take this, and the other remain on this side. However, this was not done, and at the sight of the advance guard the Zulus retire, very likely with the intention of luring us forward. Lord Chelmsford comes up and reconnoitres the ground. Then the welcome order to take the horses to water at the stream is given. How good that drink was, and how man and beast en-joyed that cool draught! The ford ia a good one though rather sandy, there is a slight incline on the other side under the foot of the bluff. The breadth of the river is about seventy yards, the water is clear and sparkling, the banks at places well wooded The bush at a little distance from the stream is not so thick, and is mostly mimosa and aloe. It was quite like seeing an old friend, seeing the Umvelosi On its head waters the column had been encamped for months, when the campaign was paralysed by the disaster of Isandula. At its source was fought Kambula, and many a time have we crossed it on different occasions since.

A troop had galloped on to secure the bluff, and had already occu-pied it, when they were recalled by Lord Chelmsford. A sharp passage of arms occurred here between Colonel Buller and a special correspondent. We fancy the latter got the worst of it, for he complained to the general, who, however, had other things to do than to rectify the wounded feelings of the hero in question.

The column encamped that night on the slope towards the river, and were for the remainder of the day engaged in clearing the bush round the camp; the spare wood was made into an "abattis" which ran outside the *laager*. Newdigate's division was higher up the slope to the rear. The night was spent in peace.

The next day we all turned out and went and had a good bathe in the clear river. Towards midday we took the horses down to water at the ford. There we found a picket; there were many men bathing all about. Just as we finished watering, a volley was poured in from the bluff, which is covered with bush, some hundred yards off. A soldier of the 90th was hit in the leg. How in the world they did so little damage we do not know. The distance was so short and the crowd so thick. The enemy had crept down and occupied every hole in the rocks possible. A lively stampede among the bathers took place. The spectacle of the naked men running about, with portions of their raiment in their hands, was most ludicrous. The picket returned the fire, we sent all the horses to the camp, and skirmished through the cover, each getting a convenient position for a shot.

A lively little fusillade ensued, the enemy firing at us and we having a shot whenever they showed. Orders were sent to retire, which was done reluctantly enough. The bathers picked up their vesture and we retired. The Zulus still held the bluff and annoyed anyone going for water by their fire. During the day the headquarter column came down to us, and their *laager* touched ours. Ours overlapping theirs gave us the advantage of a flanking fire. A stone fort was built on the top of the hill that commanded the *laager*, and some guns and a garrison occupied them. More of the brushwood was cleared away all round the camp. Large bodies of the enemy were engaged all day manoeuvring on the opposite side of the river. Several times they seemed about to cross and attack us.

Some spies were captured, one of whom we had actually employed as a butcher at Kambula, some six months previously. We do not know what was their fate. Large numbers of women were seen, through the field glasses, busily occupied burying the valuables from the various *kraals*. Further down the river, in sight, were the Opate Hills, on which the Boers had, many years previously, received such a terrible defeat. The seven military *kraals* were all in sight on the other side. Umpambongwenu the furthest off, with a broad path down it, Likazi and Ulundi next. On our right front, Indasakomi and Enokweni; right in front, Kanodwengo, the medicine *kraal*; Bulawayo and Ukandampanina on the left front. Lord Chelmsford promised Ketchwayo to spare Kanodwengo, as it was their sacred *kraal*. Generals Wood and Newdigate each sent out a spy to go to the king's *kraal* and pick up what information they could.

Night came, and the horses were got in and tied to the picket ropes. The *laager* was very crowded indeed, as both cattle and horses were inside. All had gone quietly and as usual till about ten at night, when suddenly shots were heard. We sprang up in the greatest hurry, thinking the enemy were upon us, and got our revolver from under the coat which served as a pillow. The sight that met our eyes surpasses all description, men were fighting at the foot of the slight earthwork to get in. Cries were uttered all round. Still thinking the Zulus were on us, we were looking among the struggling mass to pick out something to shoot. To our surprise we saw nothing but white men. Of course we then saw it was a scare, and got on a waggon to look round. What we saw, though ludicrous, was shameful. The demon panic was on everyone nearly.

Down the side of the *laager*, however, the 13th were in their places, steady as a rock; the 90th were falling in rapidly. The Basutos were perched upon the waggons laughing and full of excitement. The Native Irregulars were rushing into the *laager*, and were being vigorously bayoneted by the 80th, it was impossible nearly to tell them from the enemy, they were yelling like demons. At other points the sight was by no means so reassuring—men huddled together in the extremity of fear, the exertions of the officers alone prevented any firing. We saw eight men, or rather boys clinging together sobbing pitifully, while a stalwart sergeant was ordering them to their places, and banging into them with the butt-end of a rifle to enforce his commands.

Many men took refuge among the cattle and horses; a native who was guarding the cattle was there, and imagining that the enemy were attacking, stood in shade of a bullock with his shield up and *assegai* poised; the men rushing among the horses, in their turn, took him for a Zulu, and recoiled in affright. One man, who from his rank should have known better, was sleeping under a mimosa bush, he jumped up singing out, "Lord help us!" a thorn of the bush run into his side, "I am *assegaid!* I am *assegaid!*" said he, dashed over the earthwork, and tearing one man's face with his boot, jumped over the *disselboom* of the waggon and took refuge among the horses. It took some time to assure him that he was not injured.

Another man made a dive to get through the spokes of a waggon-wheel, he stuck fast, and one of the men who was on the top of the waggon rousing up, saw this below—he began at once to lay into the unfortunate fellow who roared and kicked to no purpose. Another man, three parts asleep, instead of making for the *laager* staggered into the bush until he hit his head against a stump and really got roused. Many men were stuck like the ram in the thicket in the abattis. Many tales of this sort could be told, but it is important, not on account of its ludicrous as its shameful side. Short service was here on its trial, and in a few short moments revealed more of its defects than at home in years.

The seasoned and old regiments, 90th and 13th, were ready at once; the camp could have been rushed before half the others even got their arms. We do not suppose it was from want of bravery or courage, but from no feeling of confidence in themselves that caused this. The fact is, the excessive precautions taken had made the Zulu into a regular bogie. Earthworks had been thrown up, three times as strong as our slight ones were. A regiment was constantly kept on guard with them, with us simply the pickets. One regiment on its march to join the column had *laagered* every night, even while in Natal. This might have been useful to teach them, but certainly daunted them. The men were too young altogether for the work, and though the good English stuff was in them, it wanted seasoning to bring it out. We should have suppressed this incident altogether, but it mayhap will do something to draw attention to the many grave defects in that curse of the service—short service. The rest of the night was passed peaceably.

A court-martial was held on the picket, or some men of it, and suitable punishment awarded. They had run in instead of feeling the enemy before retiring. We believe they were more afraid of their friends behind them than the enemy in front. The cause of the scare was this: the two spies sent out the previous evening had no objection to the reward, but had an objection to running any risk. Neither knew that anyone but himself was going. They went out, therefore, and after getting beyond the pickets, sat down quietly under a tree each. Wood's spy was doubtless making up a plausible tale to bring back to that officer in the morning, when he saw Newdigate's spy; he immediately shot at him and made off. Newdigate's man fired at random and ran in at the picket. The case may be *vice versâ*, but that was then the version of the affair.

This morning the Zulus again occupied the bluff, and annoyed all much. The time for the answer to the ultimatum expired at twelve. Within thirty-six hours after this the cavalry action, or skirmish of the 3rd, and the battle of Ulundi took place. At eleven orders came to saddle up, and at twelve we were in the saddle ready to dash across the river the moment the hour came.

CHAPTER 10

Towards Ulundi

At five minutes to twelve, Colonel Buller and Lord William Beresford came cantering down to us. We were halted just at the edge of the drift. This ford was some half-mile below the regular crossing. It may be remembered that the other ford was commanded by a large bluff, which rose immediately below it. This bluff fell off in a gradual decline as far as the crossing opposite to which we now stood, so that, once on the other side, a gallop of half a mile would bring us right on to the crest of the bluff, and above the enemy's sharpshooters who lined its river front. From this front, covered with rocks, had come the shots which had so annoyed us the previous day. All this edge of the river between the two fords was in sight of the *laager*, some 1,500 yards off in fact. Looking back, one could see all the waggons crowded with officers and men; everyone knew that all we did was to be done in sight of the whole column.

The object of this cavalry reconnaissance was twofold, first, to turn out those of the enemy who were in the bluff, and who had so troubled us—these were the fellows who had come down within rifle-shot of a whole army and bearded it for an entire day—the second object was to proceed as far as possible with comparative safety on the road to Ulundi, and to observe the ground most carefully on all sides; this would enable Lord Chelmsford to choose his own ground on which to fight on the morrow. We now purpose to show how these objects were effected. The colonel sat looking at his watch, as the hands pointed to twelve the order "forward" was given; plunging in, a moment or two brought us to the opposite shore; the water was shallow, not over two feet or so deep, the crossing, therefore, was easy and safe.

Immediately on gaining the opposite bank, one portion of the command turned sharply to the left, their orders were to clear the bluff and hold the other ford. By this means there would always be a retreat open to the other and larger party. This first and smaller party, with which we will cast our fortunes, consisted of about one hundred of "Baker s Horse," led by Captain and Commandant Baker. Holding to the left, they galloped up to the gentle rise along the edge of the river; the ground was pitted with holes and thick with aloes, mimosa, and other tropical shrubs, *steinbok* and *duiker* lay thick among them, and bounded up beneath our horses' feet, eyeing us with affrighted glance. The aloes through which we passed tore our clothes to pieces, however there was no time to stitch holes in clothes.

As we drew near the enemy they still made no move, and we began to suspect a trap; the fact was, the Zulus had no idea that we had crossed the stream, nor did they dream we would do so, save with a much larger force. They probably thought that the party which had moved to the lower ford merely went down to water their horses, (on each of the previous days we had done so at the same time), so moving forward quickly, and dashing through the aloes, we were among them and on to them before they were ready for us. About thirty were hastily collecting on the crest of the bluff and let fly, but in a moment went under. Running to the brow of the hill, leaving our well-trained horses to breathe themselves, just under us we saw the enemy bolting in all directions from their hiding-places in the precipitous sides. A volley makes some go down, and the others rush back again into their holes in the rocks; we scramble down and begin ferreting them out from their crannies.

As they rush out they fire hastily, we do the same, and if we miss they are shot by those of our men just above us on the verge of the precipice. One fellow we unearthed had made himself remarkably comfortable, he had got some straw to sit on, a bough bent over his head to shield him from the sun, tobacco and snuff in a crevice just beside him. He had made quite a home in this place in the rocks, and was quite protected from any fire from the *laager* side of the river; a convenient stone found him an excellent rest for his rifle, which, by the way, was a Martini. He might rest assured that from there he could beard an army and be unhurt. He fired, missed, and went under to rise no more. One fellow slipped through us and made off down the hill at a ripping pace. He passed through a shower of bullets, got cover, turned and fired, killing a horse; then off again, running the gauntlet well; just as he crossed a pool of water he was shot by Captain Baker, and fell headlong, purpling the stream with his blood. Five of the enemy took advantage of his bolt and made off toward the hills, distant some mile and a quarter.

On the top of these hills the Zulus were rapidly concentrating in dense masses. These five were pursued by the same number of Irregulars, four were lolled and one captured within rifle-shot of at least a thousand of the enemy. The prisoner was brought back, and while doing so another Zulu jumped from behind a bush, fired, missed, and died with a curse on his lips. The corps were drawn up, and preparations made to carry out Colonel Buller's order. While this was being done, the prisoner, who was secured by a valise strap round his throat, attempted to take his captor's revolver from his pocket-pouch; he had just got it out, when he was seen by a man riding behind him and shot. The prisoners were always the same, ready to sting like wasps whenever they got the chance.

A small party were sent forward to tell Colonel Buller of the massing of the enemy on his left rear; with these we will rejoin the colonel's own body of men. This consisted of the Frontier Light Horse, Mounted Infantry, Raafe's, Whalley's and the Basutos. They were in fact all that was serviceable of the Irregular Horse after a long and arduous campaign. This party had gone on in a straight line from the ford to Ulundi, then inclined to the left, so as to get on the main highway; this they did just at Kanodwengo Kraal, driving some Zulus out of it. Advancing, they found themselves in an open plain covered with long grass, which went from Kanodwengo to Ulundi, only broken by a small stream. Going forward some distance they had a perfect opportunity of seeing and observing the country, thus accomplishing the second part of the programme. Just immediately beyond this, indeed, was the ground selected for the fight of the morrow, and on this ground it was fought actually.

Here a few Zulus were seen driving a large flock of goats towards the hills. Advancing rapidly to capture these, they see a few more Zulus, one of whom Lord William Beresford pursued and overtook, and proved the superiority of the sword over the *assegai*; the man was cut down, right through shield and all, in sight of everyone. All were eager to capture the goats and bring them in, spoil of Ulundi. The vigilant colonel saw they did not appear to be in any great hurry; he immediately suspected a trap and called, "Halt and fire without dismounting, they are foxing," this was done by the leading troop, when suddenly from the grass three thousand Zulus sprung up and fired; it was a cleverly laid plot, and must have been nearly spontaneous, and was within an ace of being successful.

If there had been any dismounting, or a further advance, there would have been many killed; the enemy, who were in a semi-circle, could have rushed us before we could mount. Lying in the long grass they were completely invisible; as it was, from a volley fired at a hundred and fifty yards, only half-a-dozen men and horses were knocked over, most of the shots as usual went high. It was miraculous, yet not the less true. Here were some two or three thousand men, armed with rifles, many of them good ones, firing at some two or three hundred men at one hundred and fifty yards, and doing only so little damage; every bullet has it billet, but where these went is a wonder. The enemy poured in another volley, three men were dismounted; to one of them the adjutant of the Light Horse gave his horse, the fellow immediately rode off and left his preserver in the plain; the adjutant had extreme difficulty in escaping, of course; the man he saved and who treated him so badly was a German.

The Zulus were advancing rapidly, yet Lord William Beresford turned his horse's head and rode back, resolved to save life or lose his own. The man he went to rescue was a huge trooper of the Light Horse, his horse was shot, and he himself was giddy with pain. Here took place the scene which everyone in England knows of. On reaching, him, Lord William ordered him to mount behind him, the man either did not hear or did not understand, and hesitated; Lord William jumped off his own horse and told him if he did not mount he would punch his head; with difficulty the man obeyed and mounted behind him, and thus they rode off.

All this took place while the Zulus were racing over the one hundred and fifty yards that separated them from the pair, it, therefore, occupied but little time, enough, however, to earn two or more V.C.'s. Commandant Cecil D'Arcy, who had earned his V.C. over and over on the Zlobane day, and who, though then recommended for the decoration, did not get it as he was an Irregular, now earned it again. He likewise rode back to save a dismounted and stunned man, he jumped off his horse and attempted to lift the man bodily into the saddle, this he could not do, and while trying severely strained his back, so severely, indeed, as to have to miss the battle of the next day; probably the first fight for three years he had missed in South. Africa. The Zulus closed on him rapidly, and he was only just able, crippled as he was, to avoid them and get away, even without accomplishing his object.

The rear files of the retreating Irregulars now turned round, and began to check the pursuit of the enemy with their fire. Meanwhile an order was sent by Colonel Buller to Commandant Baker to stand firm at all hazards and keep the ford. Encouraged by the success of their comrades, the men threatening Commandant Baker descended from the hills and advanced to dislodge that officer. It became a question of time whether Colonel Buller's party could reach the ford, turning and firing as they were before Captain Baker's party were driven back, as they eventually must be. Advancing a little, Captain Baker selected a better position, halted, and began to exchange shots with the advancing enemy on his left.

Just at this moment the leading files of Colonel Buller came in sight in Baker's front, over the brow of the low eminence on which stood Kanodwengo Kraal; soon we see them all come over the brow and by the edge of the *kraal*, Colonel Buller we could see in the rear, now and then giving the word to halt and fire. Lord William Beresford was there with his just rescued man behind him, a ludicrous sight enough, two men, one of them a giant almost, mounted on Lord William's small pony. Very soon the rear files clear Kanodwengo Kraal and begin to descend the slope, the red of the mounted infantry mingled with the more sombre uniform of the Irregulars. Commandant Raafe (ably seconded by Captain Weldon, an old Central Indian man), conspicuous as usual by his splendid and cool courage; Commandant Raafe had seen many a fierce border fray in his time.

Now the advance of the Zulus appear round the corner of the *kraal*, but are saluted by such a fire that they give back; only for a moment though, for a second later they again rush forward and open into skirmishing order. Coming down the hill they are exposed to a fire from those on the opposite slope. Now the colonel's men cross the stream and begin to come up to, and pass. Baker's party, these latter still firing at the enemy on front and on the left. By this time we see that all is rights and that the colonel has again brought off his men all safe, with slight loss and a complete fulfilment of the objects of his expedition. The colonel's men cross the river and take up a position behind it to let Baker's party cross. The latter now descends from his position and rides down the path to the river; the Basutos scattered, as is their wont, everywhere, are firing furiously and at large.

With a noble disregard of the difference between friend and foe, they fire their rifles with one hand, the muzzle describing a wavering and uncertain circle embarrassing and unsatisfactory to those who, like us, were somewhere in the direction they were aiming at. One fellow, as he rode down the hill, had his rifle at the slope, and was feeding it with cartridges without ever taking it from that position. Every time the rifle went off he gave a howl of delight; how deaf he must have got with the muzzle so near his ear. We were behind this man, and between him and the enemy; he, no doubt, was something like that Scotchman, who, after Balaclava, boasted he had killed a man, but he was "no sure but it were a dam Turk."

While the last party cross the river, the water seemed to hiss and boil with the bullets from the enemy, now but a few yards off; of course your horse is thirsty and wants to drink with a most complacent disregard of danger. Once on this side the river a sort of small-arm duel begins across its flood, till an order comes down from the leader to cease firing and return to the *laager*, distant some fourteen hundred yards. A parting shot and this is done. Just as we mount a fellow steps from the tall reeds on the river's edge and deliberately fires, an officer called out "Rest your rifle in the fork of that tree and shoot that fellow," the ball struck the Zulu in the brain and he bounded into the air and fell clutching in the golden sand.

On coming in and making up the butcher's bill, the extent of the loss is seen luckily more in horse-flesh than men. There were some very ugly wounds, one man was shot just over the breast and one could see his heart beating almost. This was done by a potleg, or something of that sort; of course it proved mortal. As usual there were many narrow shaves; one man was left in the enemy's hands a prisoner, but it was of course unavoidable.

In half-an-hour the horses were out, and in an hour the men were at dinner, and the portion of the *laager* belonging to us resumed its ordinary appearance. Indeed, if a stranger went through the camp, he would not recognise the fact that the men chaffing each other and laughing away had a few minutes previously been in jeopardy of their lives. Use soon renders all callous. Some of the youngest and newest of the reinforcements came down to look at the Irregulars they had just seen engaged; they were hugely disgusted to see the men eating heartily and grunting at each other, instead of talking about their late adventure.

The rest of the afternoon passed quietly enough, rifles were cleaned and pouches refilled. Towards evening General Wood paraded his division, and told them that tomorrow he intended to cross the river, and there would doubtless be a battle, which would be fought in hollow square. He told them that the Zulus said, that as long as the 24th Regiment at Isandula fought in square nothing could be done to them. The general said that, as well he might, he had the greatest confidence in them, and told them he did not doubt the issue of the battle. This was greeted with a ringing cheer.

Arrangements were then made as to those to be left behind, the 1-24th and some others were selected for the defenders of the laager. The *laager* had been previously surrounded by an earthwork banking up the waggons to above the wheels; by this it could be defended by much fewer men, and the loss in the event of an attack would be much smaller. The shelter-trench that had previously ran round the laager was thus destroyed, and two earthworks had to be made in the four days. If the General could have only made up his mind. Throughout the whole of this war poor Tommy Atkins had to suffer for this indecision, and many a useless yard of earthwork has he ran up only to level as useless the next day. This applies more especially to the headquarter column, General Wood in ours was too careful of his men to work them thus unnecessarily.

Some spy soon took over the announcement of our crossing to the Zulus, who came down to the river and chaffed us. They told us we had been beaten that day and would be the next, that they would allow us to get well into the plain before they attacked us, and then that not a man of us would escape. We told them. "Wait a bit, old fellows, and see, mayhap it won't be so one-sided an affair as you imagine." A laugh of derision was our answer, and then they chaff away again. Soon all grows still at the river's bank, but we hear the shout of triumph and exultation swell forth as the news reaches *kraal* after *kraal*. At last the hated invader is about to hazard the final cast, tomorrow they will place themselves voluntarily in our power, and we shall be forever rich with their spoil, the men whose rifles have killed our people will now be themselves the victims. This seemed the burden of their song. It was really splendid the belief these men had in themselves.

Our feeling was something similar to a man with a good book on a race, who knows he has a real good thing on, and cannot help smiling as he sees his opponents also confident of victory. How the news got across or who was the spy was not discovered, but the news got across to the Zulus in less than an hour. All the early part of the night the enemy seemed to be marching and counter-marching from *kraal* to *kraal*, and singing their war-songs. We afterwards found out they had a big drink that night on *kaffir* beer (*utywala*). They seemed to stop a considerable time at one place, and their howls there were terrific. It seems that here they tortured and finally put to death the poor white prisoner they had taken in the morning; what his feelings must have been as the demons captured him. The *kaffir* beer looks remarkably like a certain English compound, thin gruel or skilly-go-lee, it tastes sour, but is refreshing on a hot day. The Zulus manage to get very drunk on that, and we have seen it positively running out of the mouths of some we have killed.

CHAPTER 11

The Battle

Very early in the morning our preparations are made, and long before dawn we are in the saddle and at the *drift* we crossed by at twelve on the previous day. The infantry and guns are to cross by the upper drift, a force holds the laager and the fort which commands it, with several guns also; the cattle are left in *laager* with all the sick horses, and all things left snug. It seems to be just a tossup if the Zulus will hazard all on a desperate attack on those who cross, or prefer the easier and more lucrative work of sacking, if they can, the *laager*. Each of us carry a day and half's provisions in the saddle-bag. Every man also carries one hundred rounds of ball-cartridge, there is also a large reserve of ammunition in the few waggons that accompany the infantry.

The force, crossing the river, consists of besides Irregulars, some lancers, the number we do not know, and a few dragoons as cavalry. Of artillery there were five guns of Colonel Harness's battery, all 7-pounders, two Gatlings and five guns of Major Le Grice's battery—9-pounders. The regiments were six companies of the l-13th Light Infantry; two companies of the 21st; five companies of the 80th Regiment; seven companies of the 90th Regiment; six companies of the 94th Regiment, and the 58th Regiment. We do not quite know if any of the 2-24th Regiment were there.

We soon get the order to cross the river, and in a few moments we are on the other side. We cross a little before the infantry cross at their ford. Advancing, we ride along a narrow path, which leads from our ford on to the main road. As early as we are up the vultures are ahead of us, and they rise, already nearly gorged, from the corpses of the men killed the day before. We see a good many bodies, mostly those of men wounded, and who had died after reaching the path; they had been making for the high road but had perished before getting there. The distance men will go with even such an ugly wound as a fractured knee-joint is amazing; on one occasion we came across a man who had crawled eight miles with such a wound.

On reaching the road we divide into troops, and spread out in a circle round the infantry. From our position we cannot see the latter, but know they have crossed; poor fellows, it was a bad preparation getting wet fording the river. On reaching the other side they have to get into position, which they do just beyond the bluff. The advance is again sounded, and we go on again. Our particular position was to the left front of the line of march, but a considerable distance from it. Nothing, so far, is to be seen, but a few bodies now and then marking the conflict of the 3rd. On passing Kanodwengo Kraal the enemy are seen gathering on the surrounding hills rapidly, yet keeping out of sight in a measure; for they evidently do not consider us far enough in the plain to attack us.

Many small bodies leave the *kraals* and join the various Zulus regiments concentrating on the hills. Again we halt, and looking through a field-glass at the distant enemy, are amazed to find how quickly the small companies seem to be swelling to strong regiments. Evidently there is to be a fight, but the question is will they attack us or we them. As we again proceed, they march along the hills in a line parallel to our advance. A message to the colonel gives us a chance to see what the arrangements are on the other side. The Frontier Light Horse are in front, and Whalley's and the Basutos on the right front and right. Colonel Buller is constantly going from one to another troop. On the right the same gathering of Zulus is to be seen as on the left. Instead of on the hills they are massing in the bush, and on the banks of the little river Nodwengive.

Another large body are collecting again at Ulundi. Riding back, we find that soon we shall be engaged, the enemy have left the hills and are now marching at their base. We next come across the bodies of those of our men killed by the big volley of the day before. They are naked, and have the usual Zulu *coup de grace*. Two or three horses are about, and worse than all, the body of the poor prisoner, tied to a sort of stake, and tortured and mutilated in a fearful manner. This sight is not quite the one calculated to animate one with a spirit of mercy, and threats loud and deep are uttered on the perpetrators.

Now the head of the column appears in view, just as the morning sun appears over the hills. It is a pretty sight enough that we look on, the bright steel of the bayonets, the red uniforms of the infantry, and the fluttering pennons of the lancers. Over yonder, where the Zulus are quickly gathering, all is gloom as yet; they lie under the shadow of the mountain. Now we again move forward over places where the enemy seem to have buried some of their valuables. We find the long grass in places woven together so as to trip over our horses, pits have been dug and covered over with a coarse kind of creeping grass. This was evidently done to entrap the horsemen. The square in the mean-time advances, moving briskly on—what a sight it was. The square is loose at present, but it is of such a description that a few moments could close the ranks.

The guns march parallel to the men; the regular cavalry some little distance ahead; in the centre are the ammunition waggons, water-carts and ambulances; the colours of all the various regiments are flying, the first time for many days, and the bands play them into action. The stirring music vibrates through all hearts, and makes one impatient for the battle so soon to come. Not long have we now to wait, the square nearly reaches the ground for the fight. Lord Chelmsford says to Colonel Buller, "Shall we fight here?"

"No, a little further on," is the reply.

The mass moves to the position indicated, and after some altera-tion in the formation, the guns get into position and are loaded; the ammunition boxes are opened, doctors get out their instruments, and all is ready. Will they walk into the trap? is now the question, surely it's a transparent ruse. In the meantime we are not idle, but are still in advance of the column. The Zulus now emerge from the base of the hills and strike across towards us. Looking round we see the same thing occurring on the other side. Now Colonel Buller comes up, "Send twenty men to ride up close to those fellows, and draw them on, don't let anyone dismount, and mind that donga to your right." Captain Parminter goes therefore with those twenty men, and we will go with him.

On seeing such a small band coming, the Zulus open out, and im-mediately set a trap for us. They send a body down the *donga* Colonel Buller referred to a moment ago. Even playing for such a stake as they were, they cannot help trying for even so small a trick. We ride close up to them and fire at them, more with the idea of enraging them than of doing any damage. It succeeds; furious at being bearded by so small a body, they fire at random and advance. Ah! there it is, one fellow, a pigheaded German gets down, in spite of orders, to fire. Ter-rified at the shouts and rush of the Zulus, the horse plunges and will not let its rider mount; the man himself, nervous enough now, sees the full extent of his danger. Captain Parminter rides up to him with another, and helps the man to mount; now they turn, for there's only just time to get away.

As they turn to go, the Zulus, some of whom had crept down the *donga*, redouble their exertions to cut them off, the rest of the men being safe. These last three ride at a furious pace over the ground, knowing that one false step is certain death. The place is pitted with the artificial holes dug and covered by the enemy, and the grass plaited. It seems wonderful, but these were safely crossed without mishap and again they are safe. The rifle shots resound all round the square from the Irregulars as they draw on the enemy. Effectually they have done it now, and turning they ride for the shelter of the square to avoid that storm they have raised. Very pretty the square seemed, lying there so motionless and still in the morning sun. How soon is the change to be made, and the whole face of it flash and grow pale with the volleys and smoke.

Already the artillery are at it hard, and the shells scream over our heads as we ride for the square. *Squish!* goes a rocket for Ulundi, hit it fairly as I live, and in a second a hut is in a blaze, but is quenched. The shells drop among the advancing enemy, but as they are mostly in skirmishing order the damage done is slight. A second more we are in the square, the infantry opening to let us through, we then dismount and have time to look round us. Not then did we think how pretty the square looked as we rode down to it. Within all is busy and stern. The artillerymen are standing to their guns, the infantry ready, and the cavalry standing by their horses. Down comes the advancing rush of Zulus, and now the musketry fire opens and the leaden hail sweeps the ground. By Jove, how can any living thing stand before that awful fire?

Overhead the bullets are screaming hoarsely, each with a different note. The sharper ring of the Martini plainly to be told from the duller sound of the Snider. The rough cast bullets of the Enfields and long elephant guns sing a regular *paean*, while the potlegs and wire literally howl in their course. If we are to be hit today let it be with a rifle ball if possible. The unmistakable thud of bullets as they strike horse or man is now often heard. Horses spring up into the air , as they are struck, sometimes crying in their agony. A stretcher party, the pillow already deeply dyed passes us. All things seem in pretty good form now, so we can take a walk round the square. We do so and see things worth seeing.

The position of the square may be described as follows: it was some eleven hundred yards from Kanodwengo Kraal, and about eighteen hundred from Ulundi Its front looked towards the latter and the right rested opposite the former. It was on the top of the least possible rise, but was surrounded by tall grass that much embarrassed the rifles. Just for a few yards outside the square, the grass had been hastily beaten down by the men's feet. It will be seen that it was within rifle shot of Kanodwengo Kraal. The square was constituted as follows. Its shape was oblong, one of the two shorter sides was occupied by five companies of the 80th Regiment, having two seven-pounder guns of Colonel Harness' battery placed in the centre.

The west side which was longer, was composed of the 90th Light Infantry and the 58th Regiment having two nine-pounder guns of Major Le Grice's battery in the middle. Two Gatlings were placed at the comer between the 80th and 90th Regiments. The third side, which was of the same length as that occupied by the 80th Regiment, was made up of some companies of the 21st Regiment. The lancers were immediately behind them, and two nine-pounders of Major Le Grice's battery in the centre, while another nine-pounder of the same battery separated them from the fourth side; here were stationed the 94th Regiment with six companies of the 13th Light Infantry.

Between the 94th and 13th were two of Colonel Harness' seven-pounders, and another was at the comer between the 13th and 80th. The ranks were two deep, but there was a moving chain of supports that went round as required. Some irregulars and the dragoons and mounted Basutos were drawn up behind the 80th. Each man held his bridle and stood to his horse's head. They had ample leisure to see what was going on, and their comments were most amusing. The Basutos were great fun, they had attacked the Zulus on the side between Kanodwengo and Ulundi with determined bravery and great dash. Reluctantly driven in they had come to the square and got in. At first they did not like it much, they would even have rather made a desperate effort to break through the chain of enemies.

At last they came in, and once inside their admiration was extreme. One man, Skyé by name, who spoke very good English, said, "This grand. Englishman says, come in Johnie, sit down, eatum buscuit, we fight, then make a *laager* of their own bodies, that good Englishman brave man. Englishman love poor Johnie." Having done more than their share of work hitherto, they could hardly believe all they had now to do was to look on.

At Kambula they would not enter the *laager*, but during the whole action they remained outside, and harassed the flanks of the enemy. The attitude of the miserable Natal Kaffirs or Native Contingent was in striking contrast to this. Down flat on the ground they lay, face downwards and their shields on their backs, in the most pitiable alarm, making the most hideous noises expressing their fright. Their officers were looking on and laughing at their fears, but nothing would reassure them. They were firmly convinced that their last hour was come; yet these very men that night boasted of their exploits in the most astounding way. One of the Basutos said that as they met the advance of the Zulus, the enemy called out "Now we have you at last, some few of the mounted men among you may get away, but the red soldiers will all die."

In our walk round the square we see that the ammunition waggons and water-carts are all most advantageously placed by those in charge. The doctors are busy at work with the red cross of St. George flying overhead. Army Hospital men are busy bringing them patients. Archibald Forbes, who had laid a level hundred there would be no fight, is there, looking not one whit dismayed at its loss; he stands with note-book and pencil in hand, taking in everything at a glance, and knowing probably more about the business in hand than any one there. Melton Prior is moving about also, sketch-book and pencil busily occupied, surely a picture worth drawing was he now looking on. Right well the spirit of the thing was caught, as his pictures some few weeks later proved. There too was the clergyman, Mr. Coar, who was standing at the head of a grave, quietly reading the burial service while the bullets whistled overhead.

A touching picture enough as the bodies were laid in the hastily made grave—it was a certainly unique position for an army chaplain. However necessity has no law and it may be necessary to move forward at once. There are the Gatlings just up there, working busily, making a queer clicking noise as they are fired. Let us go up and see them. There gather a few Zulus, about eighteen or so; in a moment the deadly barrels are levelled, and they disappear like a snow-wreath. A wounded artilleryman is sitting on the ground, he refuses to be removed to the hospital, but busies himself in filling the drums as they are emptied; there is his blood on the barrels of one of them where he fell after receiving his hurt.

Now comes the word passed from man to man down the ranks,

"Pass a Gatling this way," and off goes one. We heard that both went out of action afterwards from the same cause, namely the slipping out of a pin or bolt. As in both cases the pins fell into long grass, it took some time to recover them. It was a fault in the mechanism and not an inherent defect of construction, and the effect of these little weapons when held from the tops of a ship, the parapets of a fort, or in the field in position, must be wonderful. Passing through the crowded square between ambulances and ammunition waggons we see Lord Chelmsford and his staff.

Further on our own commander, Colonel Buller, with the inevitable telescope, sitting motionless on his horse. Then General Wood and his staff, next General Newdigate with his. The number of mounted officers in the square was large, and it is a great wonder that more were not hit, considering that all or the greater portion of the bullets were going high above our heads. Colonel Glyn we next see, and many other well known faces. Colonel Glyn's adjutant, or staff officer, we forget which, was hit twice while on horseback. His galloper, Lieut. Phipps, was also wounded.

Now we are again back to our place and by our horse; anyone of ours hit? No, only three horses and one trooper so far, and he only in the leg. Climbing into the saddle we get a good view of what is going forward. The long grass hides our view in a great measure, but we see the formation of the enemy plainly for all that. They seem to be in a large mass all round at various distances. A large mass is in Kanodwengo Kraal, and puffs of white smoke break from all round it. An immense body several thousands strong, are stationed at the bluff which commands the ford the infantry crossed by this morning. They are waiting there to cut us off when we shall have to break and disperse in all directions. For all we know they are going to attack the *laager* and we intently listen to hear the big guns over there; the din and roar in our position is however too great for us to catch anything.

The body of the enemy whom we had drawn on were still enduring the leaden hail and not quailing, but replying briskly. Standing up in our stirrups we can see many of the enemy quite close to us within fifty yards of the square; these the rear files, though standing up, cannot see on account of the long grass. One man we saw lying in the grass some thirty yards off, he remained motionless for about a minute while a regular tornado of bullets whizzed over his head, then he seemed to decide not to face that any longer and quietly crept back— whether he got off or not we of course do not know.

From the Ulundi direction large masses of the enemy are lying in the grass, and affording no mark save at the smoke of their volleys. They are firing briskly away, but as everywhere else, are aiming high. Now and again the bugle goes "cease firing," to let the smoke clear away, and some of the regiments are hard to stop. The fact seems to be that these very perfect and marvellously quick-shooting rifles, cause a tendency to hasty and ill-directed firing. A man has one hundred rounds of cartridge about him, and he thinks that he may fire *ad libitum*. It is simply amazing how very quickly one gets through even so large a number of cartridges. It seems a great pity that firing by volleys is not more universally carried out than it is; a really well-directed volley simply blasts and withers away everything before it, while individual firing neither does that amount of damage nor produces that moral effect that the volleys do.

Some men seemed to get so excited, those young soldiers especially so, and their officers have the utmost difficulty in making them obey the bugle call. "Look at him there, Jack, slap at him," we hear a man say. Jack obeys, though a second before an officer has spoken to him on the same subject. In some papers we read how at Ulundi whole volleys were wasted, we cannot go quite as far, though there undoubtedly was a fearful expenditure of ammunition. The number of rounds fired by our men was some thirty-five thousand exclusive of artillery fire. For this there was no corresponding return of killed enemy. Probably some twelve hundred were left dead, or in all two thousand killed and wounded, by artillery, rifles, sword and lance, and the *assegais* of the Native contingent. Looking again, we see that the enemy seem to be moving round us, outside a certain undefined sort of circle.

They appear to be looking for an opening of some sort to rush in. The bolder spirits gather for a rush, come on and are swept off or seem to melt away. Right over them we now look towards the camp, we left some days previously on the Magnumbonum heights. We know well there are many a look from there over to us and many an anxious heart as the cannons are heard from our square. A large Zulu reserve, as it appears, we see on the hills on the left, they are evidently waiting to come down and entrap us when we break Afar off over the *kraal* with a broad path down to it, Nedabakacubi by name, we see another reserve. We learned afterwards that Cetewayo and the white trader Viju were there. If we had only known it at that time we could have made a vigorous effort in that direction in the pursuit, and might have captured the king some time before he was eventually taken. He was on the direct road for the newly built Manzekane Kraal, where it was reported most of his valuables were, and which was supposed to be strongly fortified. It was distant some seventeen miles from us.

Begging a pipe of tobacco, for our own was done long before, we light up and take another walk round. An hour before we might have begged in vain for tobacco, but the knowledge that the possessor may be knocked over every minute, and the openness of heart engendered by so glorious a spectacle makes our request be gratified. Down to the ambulance we go, and see a good many men lying about, and the stretchers more bloody than they were when we saw them last; the doctors hard at work, binding up skilfully and rapidly, the *dhooly* bearers in the most abject state of funk. Here we see poor Lieutenant Pardoe of the 1-13th, a most promising officer, brought in. Soon after we go up again and see a Natal Pioneer officer get a close shave through his helmet. Colonel Drury Lowe gets knocked of his horse by a spent bullet about this time. The firing seems more rapid just now, and the enemy seem gathering for a last rush.

A sort of surging wave goes through the grass all round, is received with fearful volleys, wavers, then breaks and again opens out and begins to fire. Hurrah! that decides it all, the most determined rush is broken, and again we breathe. Now down come an order from the general. "Lancers out," the orders "stand to your horses—prepare to mount—mount," are given, and all the lancers are in their saddles. Then another piece of indecision comes, and down they get again. Another slight rush of the enemy takes place; then "Lancers out," comes again, this time in earnest. The lancers spring into the saddle, the infantry open and let them out. Down comes General Wood looking as pleased as possible to us, "All mounted men out," and in an instant we are off. The enemy halt a second, waver and then fly—the Battle of Ulundi is over and the pursuit begins.

CHAPTER 12

The Pursuit

Up into the saddle without a moment's delay, gather up the reins and pass quickly through the infantry who have done their work so well, ours is now about to begin. They give us a cheer as they wipe the perspiration that runs down their sunburnt cheeks. The Lancers, who are ahead of us, have already settled down to their work, and are riding hard with levelled lances on the fast retreating foe. We swing round to the right in the direction of the hills and lose sight of them for the time being.

All order among the enemy is gone, and they are become utterly demoralised, flying in small and scattered bands towards the hills. Soon we begin to come up with them, and the rifles once more begin to play out. Most of the Zulus on being overtaken turn round and fire, using their *assegais* immediately afterwards. Our men use their carbine pistol-wise. One has to be careful and ride with a tight rein, as every moment you pass over a body. Some living men are there too, stretched out and hiding in the long grass; they are crouched down and trusting to escape afterwards. We follow up the enemy till they reach the hills, where on the slopes they rally once more, the small bands get together and turn. A lively little bit of musketry fire takes place, which ends in the enemy retreating again, this time right to the top of the steep hill, up which it would be well nigh impossible to get. They remain there some time, and get quite numerous as each little party converges.

As we turn and ride away they give us a parting volley, they are too shaky after their long run to do much damage though. On the hillside where the grass is short we find but few bodies, and those only what we had killed in the pursuit up the slope. When, however, we arrive at the long grass, the bodies are very numerous. We spread out and hunt up those of the enemy who are hiding. They are very numerous, and a lively dropping fire is heard from both Zulu and British barrels. It is difficult to imagine why these men had not taken to their heels and bolted with their more prudent comrades. Perhaps they were so absorbed loading and firing at the square, that they had not noticed the sudden panic that ran through their ranks. Perhaps, again, they thought it was only a temporary giving back, and that at the worst they might feign death and escape when all was over. They may have crouched in abject terror, listening to the tornado of bullets that was sweeping over them, and were distraught with fear; anyhow, they died hard, fighting to the last, no cry for mercy or quarter escaped their lips.

The Basutos were very busy among them, exchanging shots at random as usual, and making things hazardous for friends and foes alike; I should think one of the most unpleasant comrades for covert shooting or grouse driving would be a Basuto, their idea of the line of fire is generous, and they distribute their bullets with charming impartiality and boundless hospitality. As the Zulus shot at them they wheeled their active little ponies and managed to escape. In one *donga* there were many Zulus hid, and the Basutos were driving them down our way. As we come close to the edge, just below our feet, we see a brawny Zulu with a muzzle-loading elephant gun resting on his knee; there seems to be something wrong, and we see him vigorously prodding away at the nipple of his piece till it gets clear.

All this time we are just above and behind him, and have him well covered with our revolvers while we watch him. Placing a cap on the nipple he climbs the opposite bank and peeps over, silently thrusting his gun forward and resting it on the edge of the *nullah*; the whole action reminds one irresistibly of deer-stalking. Just then an incautious movement on our part makes him look behind: he sees us, not soon enough to turn round and fire though, as a revolver bullet crashes through his back, and he rolls down the bank dead. Another fellow comes bounding down the *donga*, running from the Basutos, he is stooped by a dragoon or mounted infantryman, in an instant he shoots the redcoat's horse, pierces the rider through the thigh, crosses the *nullah*, stabs a doctor's horse (we believe the doctor of the 17th Lancers), a nervous start of the horse alone saving the rider from being transfixed; one moment later and the gallant Zulu falls.

The regimental dog, a cross-bred brute, who, however, is deeply enshrined in the men's hearts and affections, distinguishes himself greatly; he runs about, and whenever he comes to a living Zulu barks at him furiously. This is very useful, as many are simply shamming dead or foxing in the grass, they will take a pot shot at you the moment your back is turned. The old dog will not even look at a really dead Zulu, but if one is foxing a good bite soon raises him to fury and to a headlong attack on poor 'Lion'; who has a tolerable eye to his own safety. Turning again to the square we pass a Zulu, lying to all appearance dead, with two magnificent *assegais* and a gun beside him; Captain Baker says: "Jump down and get those for me," the moment the *assegais* are touched the fellow springs up, levels his gun and fires, missing his mark and killing Lieutenant Addie's horse.

The effects of the shell fire was marked in the extreme, here and there we came across the most fearfully mutilated bodies; the rockets also seemed to have inflicted terrible wounds. The dead, on the other hand, who were slain with the Martini rifles were singularly little disfigured, a very small hole where the bullet went in, and another rather larger at the exit were the only marks.

Everything was by this time over, and we quietly follow in the wake of Colonel Buller towards Ulundi. Down by the little Ulundi River we dismount to get a draught of water, as we stoop down to drink we see, a foot from us, a Zulu, standing in the water with his head hidden by the overhanging rushes. It rather startles one as you are just getting a gulp of the much needed water, to see a hideous face so close. Search shows five more of these fellows in the same pool, and as they refuse to yield the water is soon undrinkable and bloody. Long after we hear shots, as the pools are searched the one after the other by the native contingent. These last, after the most abject and pitiful terror during the fight, had mustered courage enough to rush out of the square after the horsemen, a few Zulus turned on them, and despite the exertions of their European leaders they had bolted, only to come out again when everything was done except slaughter.

We were all moving again leisurely towards Ulundi, in rear of Colonel Buller, when he suddenly turned round and sang out: "Now, then, who's first into Ulundi?" waiving his own undoubted right to first footing. Immediately we dash off for the *kraal*, distant some quarter of a mile or so. Lord William Beresford leads, and going straight as a dart for the stiff fence round the *kraal*, his little pony flies it like a bird, landing cleverly in among the beehived shaped huts. Others more prudent make for the top side of the *kraal*, where stands the large square mud house, the late residence of His Majesty King Ketchwayo. Up to this we race, and jumping off, rush through the opening and find ourselves in a sort of labyrinth made of tall stiff wooden fences, over which it is impossible to climb. This was evidently built to guard against a surprise; it stretches all round the royal house, and might be held for a long time by a handful of resolute men against a foe who was not possessed of artillery. Clearly he who made it never contemplated its use, save against a sudden rising of his clans; the floor it was erected on was of clay hardened like cement, and was clean swept

A lucky hit off of the right passage brings us to the door just behind Captain Baker; Lord William Beresford was running towards the door from another direction, and though first in the *kraal*, he was not foremost at the palace, if one may stretch a point and dignify it by that name. It was a low single-storied house built of mud-bricks, or mud and wattle. It contained eight rooms, and had a steep thatched roof, that the rockets had touched but not burnt. A vigorous kick by Captain Baker to the rude unpainted door and we are inside, and see— well not Ketchwayo, who we dreamed might possibly have been there. The whole floor was covered with dead men, not flesh and blood though, but only Champagne and square face (Geneva or Hollands) bottles lying about in confusion. Two springs and we seize one, alack! alack! it is empty, another and yet another tell the same tale, and we see that the El Dorado that had opened for us has vanished; but what a royal booze poor Ketchwayo must have had with all this.

We afterwards found out that he had had a tremendous *carouse* the night before with his chiefs and leaders, indeed, tradition says the royal toper, albeit a good and seasoned bibber, got "*vara fou*" that night; poor fellow, a lost battle, a lost kingdom and a hurried flight were not the best of pick-me-ups the next morning. However, there they were, but, as I live, one with the cork untouched and the gold seal intact, Heidseck's Dry too, just right, alas! through a small crack its contents have long since vanished. Put it down, plenty of others will be sold the same way as yourself

On first entering Captain Baker stumbled over two bits of wooden-like substance and kicked them out of his way; Lord William Beresford picks them up, and we see they are two elephants' tusks, only one other is taken, and that a small one, which Captain Baker keeps. A large box or locker stands in a corner, a kick opens it; one does not stand on ceremony when looting. It is found full of old newspapers. *Illustrated London News, Times, Standard, Graphic,* and many Colonial papers, Dutch and English, these latter all containing references to the Zulus and Ketchwayo; some were five years old, and they contained all the doings of the Boundary Commission, the Ghaika and Galeka War, Secocoeni's war, the annexation of the Transvaal, comments on the Zulu Army and war-like intentions of Ketchwayo, everything tending to give him an idea of how frightened the Colonists were of him. Then there was an illustration of his coronation by Shepstone. Ketchwayo was certainly not as ignorant of the white man's intentions as is supposed, here was a Colonial version, with comments for years on all his actions; they were much worn and thumbed over.

The English papers, especially the illustrated ones, were very old, one of the oldest being an *Illustrated London News* with all the pictures of the marriage of the Prince of Wales. How strange it seemed to look on the features of the best loved face in England in the midst of barbarism, and after looking on the scenes we had witnessed one short hour before. Her Majesty opening Parliament, scenes in the Russo-Turkish War, the Franco-Prussian War, some few pictures of the old Colony War. One of these must have roused his phlegm considerably, it was "Kaffir Prisoners entering King William's Town," and represented some miserable-looking *Kaffirs* escorted, with hands bound behind their backs, by mounted volunteers. Many others were found, too numerous to mention.

Leaving the house, we found a troop starting off to burn a *kraal* still further on, the writer was ordered by Colonel Buller to commence to burn the royal *kraal*, which he did with Captain Prior of the 80th (now Major) and Captain Parminter. By these three the 10,000 huts which made up Ulundi were burnt, no one else assisting or being near. The huts were nearly a mile round, and were dry and burnt well. The burners rode from hut to hut with flaming torches of grass, and after hard work got everything in flames. The huts were small and bad, save those round the king's house for his chief wives, the others were decidedly the worst huts we had seen in Zululand. At the bottom corner there was a splendid pile of skins ready to make into shields.

After the burning is over we have some time to rest, and go about looking for loot, a freshly turned up piece of soil attracts us, and sticking the assegai we happen to have into the ground it rings on iron, further investigation reveals a large slab of iron, evidently the lid of a safe; at last all is right, and our fortunes are made, we think; that fortune so oft delayed, so long sought for. At last we find out our safe turns out to be a large American cooking stove, planted in the ground about a foot deep. Still we think it must contain valuables, and pulling the boiler lid off discover—what? well, about the last thing we expected to see, a set of blacking-brushes. Cruel irony, that condemned us to see our own hopes so shattered, and by so ridiculous an ending.

Whatever could a Zulu do with blacking-brushes, he could not brush his boots for the sufficient reason that he had none to black. His own skin was black enough, and sleek and shiny not to require polishing, so what could we do with them? It's a conundrum we have often puzzled over; we have the brushes yet. After this we sit down, and in sight of the still blazing huts share the last bottle of champagne left us in the world. For four long months have we cherished that bottle to keep to celebrate the event we are now witnessing; through many dangers it had passed safely, and delicious was it now. We then write a hurried note or two to be sent off to friends in England, to be posted by the post that we know will leave camp tonight, letters, by the bye, that they never got.

It would little boot to tell of the other adventures that befell us, suffice to say that we got back to the square; had a scrambling sort of a lunch, and were then sent off to cover a party of Shepstone's Basutos, who were dispatched to burn some distant *kraals*. As we went, we rode over a different part of the field by the Kanodwengo Kraal, and saw some bodies of mules and horses that lay dead, killed by our shells, their riders evidently were laying behind the *kraal* in wait to pounce on the stragglers when the square was shattered by their men's fierce attack We forgot to say that after the pursuit, and before we went to the *kraal*, we covered some guns that were sent to dislodge the Zulus, who were in the mountain where we had driven them, the shells just pitched well into them as they sat looking at us, making them again fly. Some Basutos we saw here, said that many of the people killed by these shells were women, who had been looking at the fight from the hills. At five we got back to camp thoroughly done up, having had a hard day.

It would interest no one to know how we left the banks of the Umvelosi River the next day, though the burial of Captain Wyatt Edgehill's body on the night of the battle down by the riverside was an impressive sight, buried as he was by his sorrowing comrades in the dead of night.

We arrived at Magnumbonum heights on the 6th of July, Newdigate's Column having arrived on the 5th. The change of temperature was great from the warm vale to the bleak hills, it made us very glad to get once more under canvas. We were also rejoiced to see a "smouch waggon," and cheerfully paid enormous prices for such luxuries as sardines, jam, preserved salmon, &c.

Our comrades, left behind on the hill, had watched the battle anxiously on the 4th. The rain delayed us at Magnumbonum three days, such rain, cold as ice, and that killed off our poor draught bullocks and horses literally by the dozen; all round the camp were they lying. On the 10th we left the camp, and had tremendous work to collect and account for all our horses, the fog and rain had driven some miles away; they had broken loose from the picket-lines and got lost in the fog. One raid had been made on the 7th by Colonel Buller, he started with a couple of troops at three a.m., and riding a whole day in the fearful rain returned to camp with a fine herd of captured cattle.

On this patrol the lightning struck the ground close to us, and though the rank grass was saturated with rain burned a piece clean off. A ration of rum was served out on the 8th inst. to all hands, in honour of the victory. On the 11th we turned off the old road by which we advanced and reached a beautiful mission station, Quamagasa, formerly the residence of Bishop Robertson. It was a lovely spot, closely planted with trees, off which we got a quantity of lemons, the gardens also were full of Cape gooseberries, but were soon desolate. Here was found the body of Lieutenant Scott Douglas, the signalling officer, with the body of Corporal Cotter of the 17th Lancers, who escorted him. They had been missing some days, having ridden from Magnumbonum to the next fort, and returning in the fog it is conjectured they lost their way, and falling in with Dabulamanzi's people were killed.

The corporal had evidently fought hard, as traces of a terrible struggle were seen all round; they had been surprised while resting under a tree. In the evening they were buried. Neither of the bodies were mutilated in any way. On the 13th we left Quamagasa and arrived at St. Paul's Mission Station on the 15th, where Sir Garnet Wolseley joined us. The next day the flying column was reviewed. We had parted from Newdigate's some days previously. As our orders were to turn out as strong as possible, the blind, the maim, and the halt among the horses were brought out for the march past. All day long on the 16th the natives were bringing in guns, all Enfields, but no Martinis.

On the 18th there was a parade, a speech from Colonel Buller and General Wood to say goodbye. The latter was loudly cheered, but the colonel came in for such an ovation as he will probably never forget, and which moved him enough to make his voice tremble as he wished all goodbye. Long after he went did we follow his figure as it went up the hill from us. After his departure the interest in everything was over, as he was the life and soul of the column. Many an Irregular read with honest pride the enthusiastic welcome that England gave to Sir Evelyn Wood and Colonel Buller, our leader and beloved chief. Not a few but owed their lives to the latter, and right glad we were to see that he got the C.M.G. and was made A.D.C. to the Queen, honours well deserved by him surely. Sir Evelyn also had still further proved his undoubted ability and made his name.

The Frontier Light Horse, our gallant comrades, also went on the 18th from the column. We ourselves left the day after, and in a few days the flying column was no more. The 13th Light Infantry left on their way to England, the 90th Light Infantry left for India, the 80th were to remain in the country. For ourselves we were to march down to Durban and there disband. So we were to be scattered to the four corners of the earth, and that division in which from highest to lowest a spirit of cordial admiration, obedience and loyal co-operation had reigned, was to be broken up.

Our orders were to march *via* Ekowe and Fort Tenedos. As soon as we left St. Paul's we descended into a thickly wooded, luxuriant tropical country, full of game of all sorts, and reported to contain buffalo. The ground was deep and heavy, and the country impassable on either side of the road. The few *kraals* were full of natives, who seemed cheerful and good-natured, ready to sell fowls and doubtless wondering why [we took the trouble to pay for them. Many had terrible scars which they were fond of showing. That evening we camped by the Umletosi River, and had a good bathe spite of the crocodiles it was supposed to be full of. We also caught some fish, like *barbel*.

On the 21st we reached the Umlalas River, after a tiring march during which we lost ten oxen. There was a fort at Umlalas garrisoned by a fever-stricken detachment of the 88th Connaught Rangers. Poor fellows, we had seen them at Durban, but very different they looked then to what they did now after months of inaction, camped in pestilent marshes. The fact is the authorities had accumulated so many tons of stores there, someone must eat them, so despite fever the 88th stayed there, and did their best, with but little appetites for the task before them. Someone had blundered, and the poor 88th had to pay and eat for it.

The next day we saw Ekowe, with its large and strong earthworks. No Zulus could have taken it. It was a very pretty spot, and was formerly a mission station. Around it lay the graves of those who had died during Pearson's occupation of it.

103

The next day we passed down from the hills again, passing many waggons abandoned by Pearson on the 23rd of January after his fight at Ineyzane. The battlefield of Ineyzane we also rode over and inspected, it was like a very thickly wooded park, with reeds instead of grass. The fight must have been a scramble in the dark for everyone, both Zulus and English, and the only wonder is that a disaster similar to Isandula did not take place. The train of waggons was of immense length, imperfectly guarded, and if the Zulus had attacked the waggons instead of the advance guard, we do not see what was to avert a catastrophe. We saw the graves of those who fell, under a spreading tree by the roadside, just where the slope begins. We caught some capital fish in the Ineyzane brook, a sluggish river, we ate them undisturbed by the thought that they may in their turn have feasted on the Zulus who fell there at the fight.

For some days we had some capital sport shooting partridges, deer, &c., and on the 22nd of July reached Fort Tenedos. The fort at the Zulu side of the river was Fort Tenedos, the one at the Natal side was Fort Pearson, both were very strong. Too strong to be taken by Zulus. A small town had sprung up around the fort, inhabited by innkeepers, storekeepers, bakers, &c. We were soon deep in the delights of civilized luxuries, they were rather dearer than at home it is true, yet how much better beer tasted there than at home; heat and long fasting probably did it, at all events I know that our first draught went down as beer never went before, or will hardly do again, till some future war calls us out again to once more work for it. We passed quickly through the sugar-growing and beautiful sea-coast of Natal and arrived at Sacchrine Railway Station on the 31st of July.

On the 2nd the Regiment was run down past Durban and put on board the *City of Venice* to be disbanded, some were to be put ashore at Port Elizabeth, some at Capetown. We bid goodbye with unfeigned regret to our comrades in arms, who though rough and rude were good men and true at heart. For months previously officers and men had pulled together well and willingly. All were sorry to part, and often was the Commandant preferred service if he would raise a corps to fight Secocoeni. All partings come to an end, and at last we leave with Captain Baker and turn our faces again to Natal, followed by the ringing cheers of our late troopers. Here endeth that corps yclept Baker's Horse, who after many months of gallant service were once more dispersed to the winds, where are they now, we wonder? like the old stave I should think, "*Some are dead and more are gone, and others beyond the seas got scraped to death with oyster shells, among the Carribees."*

It is hard lines that after Captain Baker's long and gallant service, he should have got simply nothing out of it. The winding up of this corps financially too was done better than any other Irregular corps. At least he might, in the lavish distribution of honours that took place, have got a C.M.G., or better still that honorary lieutenant-colonel-cy he coveted. Certainly not a man in South Africa deserved some recognition of arduous service more than he did, and we hope that those merits will yet be recognised by the War Office. His were the first reinforcements to reach Lord Chelmsford after Isandula when the colony stood in most need of them. That officer, however, did not even take the trouble to thank Commandant Baker, though the corps were raised with incredible celerity by dint of Captain Baker's personal popularity in Port Elizabeth. We are afraid your readers will be out of patience with our growl, but it is riling to see merit passed over, and mediocrity rewarded.

So ends the Chronicles of the Irregular Horse, the other corps were quickly broken up, save the Frontier Light Horse who went up against Secocoeni, and were disbanded on the 26th of January, 1880, after a long and honourable career. Captain Walley's corps was broken up in August, 1879. Commandant Raafe's in August also, the last named officer received a C.M.G. The Irregulars were a force, taken altogether, which did the work intrusted to them well, though roughly, and it is a pity they were not made into a permanent force. However those in authority know best, and now for Northward Ho! and Home.

CHAPTER 13

The Boer Outbreak

The following may now be of interest to the readers. It is a short sketch of the revolt in the Transvaal, or rather some short observations on it. It is the work of one particularly well qualified, from a residence of several years to speak on the subject. These years, or rather the latter portion of them, were spent on active service in and near the Transvaal. The earlier portion was spent in the Cape Colony, in various districts inhabited by Dutch settlers, and in service there.

In the first place let us state the case of the Boers, which is simple. They allege that the British government forcibly took possession of their country: that they used every means in their power to get redress, and that after waiting patiently three years, finding other means unavailing they had been obliged to resort to armed resistance. This is their whole case, which appears to have excited the sympathy of a large section of the English public. The contention on the other side is, that the Transvaal was a country in a state of anarchy and bankruptcy, without any means of maintaining its frontier against the attacks of savages, who unopposed were taking possession of the territory of the Republic, and who threatened to become dangerous to the British colonists.

Therefore Shepstone went to Pretoria, and declared the South African Republic no longer independent but annexed to Great Britain. There was but little force displayed on this occasion. Sir T. Shepstone's force was but 28 men, they could have been destroyed and made prisoners in a few minutes. Such is the case on which the Boers have at last joined issue with the Imperial government. We think careful consideration of facts will eliminate any sympathy for the ill-advised Dutchmen. Here we wish to record an opinion that 4-5ths of the population of the Transvaal were well disposed to British rule. At least such is the results of our observations and an interchange of ideas with the most respectable portions of the Dutch community. Many of the Boers in the Transvaal have immigrated there from the Cape Colony, and not a few since the annexation. We had a good opportunity of knowing many Dutch farmers in the old Colony and their reasons for moving.

Some were not doing well owing to unfavourable conditions of soil and climate; losses of stock through disease and draught and other causes independent of forms of government, others were lazy and good-for-nothing-rascals who would prosper nowhere. Again there were Boers who had not sufficient elbow room, for it is the great ambition of these to be able to stand on some elevated spot near their houses, and point out the extent of their domains. We who wish to make the farms smaller are consequently disliked, and it is rather like the squatter and free selector question in Australia. An adverse judicial decision would set such to brood over their wrongs. They would accept an offer for land and stock and forthwith "*inspan*" their waggons, and "*trek*" off to join Burgers as they expressed it.

The main cause of complaint was the degree of freedom enjoyed by the natives. For many years after the Cape was ceded by the Batavian General Janusens, slavery was recognised by the British Government. According to all accounts the Hottentot and other native bondsmen had a very miserable time. There are extant painful records of flogging, tortures, and destruction of life. The bushmen who resolutely refused to enter a life of slavery were shot down by the Dutch as we shoot vermin. The Roman Dutch law certainly did not sanction these barbarities. Few, however, of their perpetrators were ever brought to trial, and if they were, justice was satisfied by the imposition of a small fine.

At the present time, (as at time of first publication), the Boer says that a native can commit any crime with impunity. They say under British rule the magistrate always favours the black man. There is some truth in this statement. The heaviest sentence we ever saw passed on a native for sheep-stealing was six months' imprisonment. When we consider that the great business of stock raising is carried on in a country destitute of fences, and with little or no police surveillance, it is an inadequate punishment. We believe that this unrestrained vagabondage of the natives and their almost entire immunity from punishment is the chief cause of discontent in the Boer mind.

In the Orange Free State, and also in the Crown Colony of Natal, the natives are kept within bounds by very salutary regulations. They are not allowed to be out after a certain hour in the evening, and, moreover, the sale of intoxicating liquors, to them, is forbidden. Beyond this native question, we know of no other genuine grievance of the Boers to our rule. We have said that we consider 4-5ths of the Dutch population favourable to British rule in the Transvaal. This opinion Colonel Lanyon, our ablest African administrator, has also expressed in his dispatches.

The opponents of our annexation are a certain class of political agitators, with little or nothing to lose; not all of them Dutch by any means. Indeed we are convinced that a good number of Englishmen of broken fortunes with no ostensible means of support, attracted originally to South Africa by the Diamond Fields, where they have spent their time hanging about canteens and hotel bars, will be found to have taken part in stirring up the present commotion. On these Diamond Fields were at one time a certain number of Irishmen of advanced views who openly proclaimed their hostility to the British government. The tactics of the Boers are indeed very much the same as those followed by the Irish agitator, during the last three or four months, and if we do not mistake we shall hear soon from the Transvaal of the same coercion terrorism and violence that are now reported daily in Ireland. From this class of needy agitators it is but just to except men like Paul Kruger and Joubert, fanatics of the Calvinist school, who, we are firmly convinced, are acting sincerely up to their convictions.

However this may be, war has broken out and British authority set at defiance. The first step of course is to quench the rebellion as soon as possible. That the Boers can make any protracted stand against regular troops is impossible, and we doubt very much whether they will make the attempt. Behind intrenchments, if they have the art to make them, they will fight, as also in the natural positions so plentiful in the spurs of the Drakensburg mountains. No resistance that these men could make will prevent the passage of a column of troops sufficiently strong and ably led from Natal into the Transvaal either by the Coldstream and Mark's store route which is the most difficult or by the Newcastle and Utrecht road across the Buffalo, which passes through an open country where artillery can have full play.

That they may make much trouble by attacks on convoys is evident and also by cutting telegraph wires and interrupting communications generally. Furthermore by setting their backs to the Vaal River and by alternately advancing and retiring to their friends in the Free State the war may be protracted indefinitely, unless Mr. Brand's government be compelled by threats of retribution to make its subjects observe neutrality. The Boer as a rule is not a courageous man, and will not fight unless driven into a comer whence there is no escape. As they are all mounted and good horsemen this last operation is impossible, and none of our regular cavalry could ever hope to gain anything by a pursuit.

When hard pressed by want of supplies they will return to their houses (where by the way they have left their families) and have a period of rest, telling any of the British patrols visiting them that they have taken no part in hostilities or that they were forced from home against their will. It is to be a matter of some difficulty to deal with people adopting these tactics which were to my knowledge followed most successfully by the insurgent natives near the mission stations in British Kaffraria. That the rebellion must be suppressed with a high hand effectually is a matter admitting of no question, if we wish to maintain our supremacy in South Africa. The native races have seen the Imperial troops victorious in all conflicts with themselves and know that when the red coats appear on the scene their thorough subjugation is only a matter of time.

We are quite convinced that the presence of a few hundred troops in Basuto land would effect more in a week than all Mr. Sprigg's motley crowds of colonists and irregulars have accomplished (if they have accomplished anything) in six months. For the benefit of the Zulus and other powerful tribes it must therefore be shown clearly that white antagonists to British supremacy will also be speedily brought to their senses.

The rebellion suppressed, the next question that arises is the future of the Transvaal. First and foremost, however, comes the duty of dealing out stern retribution to those concerned in the murder of British subjects or of people in the pay of the Imperial Government. Mr. Kruiger's administrators will certainly disavow any connection with these murderers who have probably ere this taken refuge in the Free State, which should be compelled to give them up for punishment by court martial. Public opinion in England seems to demand that the question of annexation shall be reconsidered—with a view to determine whether the Transvaal should not be re-transferred to the Republic. If it be so determined, the Boers should be made to pay either in money or in territory their quota of the expenses of the Zulu War, and the whole of those incurred in the operations against Secocoeni; and, furthermore, a force should be retained in the country, and at its expense, until this indemnity be paid, and the security of the lives and property of those adhering to the British rule in the present struggle guaranteed for the future.

These terms are demanded by common justice. The wars of 1878-80 were nothing but a source of emolument to the Boers for whose protection they were undertaken. With the exception of a few frontier farmers who joined General Wood, after having been obliged to abandon their houses, the assistance rendered by the other Boers was limited by supplying transport at most exorbitant charges. They made also demands for imaginary damages committed by Imperial forces passing near their deserted farms, and were not backward in clamouring for compensation on account of lost or dead oxen that had never left the claimants' farms.

The Colonists of English descent, it must be admitted, were also equally conspicuous in rendering this sort of assistance to the Government in its need. We observe that £250,000 will be paid by Natal towards the expenses of the Zulu War, and at least half this sum should be demanded from the Transvaal if it be restored to the Republican Government. It was, moreover, currently asserted that the Boers were in communication with Cetywayo before the outbreak of, if not during the war. Whether this be true or not, it seems established that they have instigated the Basutos and other natives to rise against the Cape. When we remember that Ketywayo asked Mr. Shepstone to let him have "just one little war," and "wash his *assegais*" in the Transvaal, then ruled by Mr. Burgers, and that he was persuaded by that official to relinquish his designs on the Boers, it will readily be understood that these Republicans have alienated the goodwill and sympathy of all honest men and well-wishers to South African progress.

We have mentioned once or twice that the majority of the Dutch residents are well disposed towards British rule, and we would suggest that it be ascertained, when the war is over, whether this disposition cannot be proved to the satisfaction of those ill-informed people in England and elsewhere that are crying out at the top of their voices for justice to the Dutch. We do not know of any country where the subject enjoys the same degree of liberty as in the Transvaal under British rule. The law as expounded by Dutch *jurisconsuls*, is identical with that observed by Riebeck and his settlers in 1667, is administered by Dutch judges and magistrates, almost all of whom held office under the Republic.

The taxation, mostly indirect, is just sufficient to maintain these officials, and is far less grievous than that imposed by the Republican government. It must be said, however, that this latter executive did not recover payment from those who thought proper not to contribute their share of the public revenue; a happy-go-lucky system which brought the country to ruin. Moreover, under the British rule the Boers' life and property were secure from attacks, a somewhat novel experience to those living on the eastern and northern borders, which they have not been backward in appreciating.

We should think it would be easy to determine the opinion of the majority by a species of plebiscite, or census carried out by enumerators of strict impartiality, and bound over to secrecy. Let the question be put to every Dutchman holding property of any description, "Do you wish for British rule or for the Republic?" Let every man give his vote on these questions according to his conscience, being previously assured that his decision will never be divulged even to his wife and chi dren, and we are very much astonished if the results of this balloting would not forever and a day close the mouths of noisy agitators and so-called politicians never weary crying down their own country, and criticising those who carry out their duties firmly and faithfully.

There are at present in the north of the Transvaal whole districts once occupied by farmers and their stocks that are now abandoned to the encroaching natives. The disappearance of the British flag from the Transvaal will be the signal for the adjacent native races to overrun the whole Republic and satisfy long-standing grudges. The Boers have shown their inability to meet these invasions, and a complete want of unanimity and patriotic spirit. Fighting the British Government and the native tribes are two very different things as they know. That they incur little risk in conflict with a civilised nation, which will simply content itself with dispersing armed resistance without interfering with private property, is shown by the large numbers of men they have, with the assistance of the Free State, put into the field. A war with a native tribe means loss of life and property, everything being destroyed except the women who would probably be left to starve, possibly worse.

Whether we are justified in abandoning the country to this fate even at the request of its inhabitants is a knotty point which will cause much anxious consideration to philanthropists and statesmen. The Colonial office possessing as it does such unrivalled sources of information, and advised by men like Sir Owen Lanyon, can be safely depended on to settle the matter in a way alike honourable to the nation and in a manner satisfactory to the misguided Boers. The experience of the office in our vast colonial affairs will enable them to devise the best means to that end. Let us hope Lord Kimberley's efforts will be crowned with success.

In considering the Boer question, it should be considered that their position is different to any other nation in the world. With them there are no separate classes. All occupy the same position, that of owners of land, and are all equal. The stores are all in the hands, of Europeans. From their childhood, their wandering instincts are fostered by the very manner of their life. Once a year or so, they go off with their parents, and are absent from home, leading a vagabond's existence "on trek" for two or three months. This causes them to be unsettled and fond of change, and the same spirit moves them in their relations to the Government. With railways and increased civilization, this feeling will disappear and they will become attached to our rule.

As for the agitation now being got up for the Boers by the Hollanders, it is absurd. No doubt blood is thicker than water, but a carrying back of the Hollanders' sympathy to a people who left Holland some two hundred years ago, is as if in the event of a war between the United States and some power we agitated in favour of the States. Doubtless we should wish them well, but should stop short at that—carry the principle further, and we may expect to see Greece agitating against Italy's suppression of the Sicilian brigands, because Sicily was a Grecian Colony.

As to the carrying on of the war, it is simply a question of a chain of posts and cavalry raids under some experienced leader like Colonel Buller. These raids will serve to show the Boers how completely their homes are in our power, and will speedily bring them to their senses. Regular cavalry as now armed are of small use against the Boers. Firstly, Boers' horses are the best; secondly, Cavalry carbines carry 600 yards, Boers' rifles 1200, result—the Boers can keep 800 yards away and can simply pour in shot after shot without reply. Their extreme mobility will always keep them out of range of cavalry. On being charged they will disperse and fly. Their knowledge of the country will always enable them to avoid being trapped.

Unless we have experienced officers and trustworthy guides the same rule will not apply to us. Regular cavalry horses cannot stand an arduous campaign with the weight they now carry. Irregulars who fight the Boers with their own weapons and tactics are the true remedy. Man for man they are the Boers' equals, and the good English pluck they have to boot, will carry them through victorious.

The mere threat of calling in Zulus and Swazies would oblige the Boers to submit at once.

We question if it would be advisable to give up the Transvaal. In 1854 being in want of men for the Crimean campaign, we withdrew the 500 men who garrisoned the now Orange Free State, and gave it up to the Boers. Now the Transvaal Boers use it as a rallying point in their operations against us.

To us, Africa should become a second India, and should be British from Table Bay to Cape Guardafui. Such it will be, spite of all the clamour from a section at home. The same cry that ruined Clive and Warren Hastings, ruined Sir Bartle Frere. History will do equal justice to his career in the future, as it has done to Clive and Hastings. To a barbarism a thousand fold greater than that of India, we are the pioneers of Christianity and civilization. Should we pause in our glorious career?

LEONAUR

ALSO FROM LEONAUR

AVAILABLE IN SOFTCOVER OR HARDCOVER WITH DUST JACKET

"AMBULANCE 464" ENCORE DES BLESSÉS *by Julien H. Bryan*—The experiences of an American Volunteer with the French Army during the First World War

THE GREAT WAR IN THE MIDDLE EAST: 1 *by W. T. Massey*—The Desert Campaigns & How Jerusalem Was Won---two classic accounts in one volume.

THE GREAT WAR IN THE MIDDLE EAST: 2 *by W. T. Massey*—Allenby's Final Triumph.

SMITH-DORRIEN *by Horace Smith-Dorrien*—Isandlwhana to the Great War.

1914 *by Sir John French*—The Early Campaigns of the Great War by the British Commander.

GRENADIER *by E. R. M. Fryer*—The Recollections of an Officer of the Grenadier Guards throughout the Great War on the Western Front.

BATTLE, CAPTURE & ESCAPE *by George Pearson*—The Experiences of a Canadian Light Infantryman During the Great War.

DIGGERS AT WAR *by R. Hugh Knyvett & G. P. Cuttriss*—"Over There" With the Australians by R. Hugh Knyvett and Over the Top With the Third Australian Division by G. P. Cuttriss. Accounts of Australians During the Great War in the Middle East, at Gallipoli and on the Western Front.

HEAVY FIGHTING BEFORE US *by George Brenton Laurie*—The Letters of an Officer of the Royal Irish Rifles on the Western Front During the Great War.

THE CAMELIERS *by Oliver Hogue*—A Classic Account of the Australians of the Imperial Camel Corps During the First World War in the Middle East.

RED DUST *by Donald Black*—A Classic Account of Australian Light Horsemen in Palestine During the First World War.

THE LEAN, BROWN MEN *by Angus Buchanan*—Experiences in East Africa During the Great War with the 25th Royal Fusiliers—the Legion of Frontiersmen.

THE NIGERIAN REGIMENT IN EAST AFRICA *by W. D. Downes*—On Campaign During the Great War 1916-1918.

THE AUXILIA OF THE ROMAN IMPERIAL ARMY *by G.L. Cheeseman*

THE MILITARY SYSTEM OF THE ROMANS *by Albert Harkness*

LEONAUR

ALSO FROM LEONAUR

AVAILABLE IN SOFTCOVER OR HARDCOVER WITH DUST JACKET

THE ART OF WAR *by Antoine Henri Jomini*—Strategy & Tactics From the Age of Horse & Musket.

THE ART OF WAR *by Sun Tzu and Pierre G. T. Beauregard*—*The Art of War* by Sun Tzu and *Principles and Maxims of the Art of War* by Pierre G. T. Beauregard.

REVOLT IN THE DESERT *by T. E. Lawrence*—An account of the experiences of one remarkable British officer's war from his own perspective.

THE BENGAL NATIVE ARMY *by F. G. Cardew*—An Invaluable Reference Resource.

ARTILLERY THROUGH THE AGES—*by Albert Manucy*—A History of the DEvelopment and Use of Cannons, Mortars, Rockets & Projectiles from Earliest Times to the Nineteenth Century.

THE SWORD OF THE CROWN *by Eric W. Sheppard*—A History of the British Army to 1914.

THE 7TH (QUEEN'S OWN) HUSSARS: Volume 3—1818-1914 *by C. R. B. Barrett*—On Campaign During the Canadian Rebellion, the Indian Mutiny, the Sudan, Matabeleland, Mashonaland and the Boer War Volume 3: 1818-1914.

TIGERS ALONG THE TIGRIS *by E. J. Thompson*—The Leicestershire Regiment in Mesopotamia During the First World War.

RIFLE & DRILL *by S. Bertram Browne*—The Enfield Rifle Musket, 1853 and the Drill of the British Soldier of the Mid-Victorian Period *A Companion to the New Rifle Musket* and *A Practical Guide to Squad and Setting-up Dtill.*

FARAWAY CAMPAIGN *by F. James*—Experiences of an Indian Army Cavalry Officer in Persia & Russia During the Great War.

THE WOMAN IN BATTLE *by Loreta Janeta Velazquez*—Soldier, Spy and Secret Service Agent for the Confederancy During the American Civil War.

THE BUSH WAR DOCTOR *by Robert V. Dolbey*—The Experiences of a British Army Doctor During the East African Campaign of the First World War

PERSONAL RECOLLECTIONS OF JOAN OF ARC *by Mark Twain.*

CAESAR'S ARMY *by Harry Pratt Judson*—The Evolution, Composition, Tactics, Equipment & Battles of the Roman Army.

FREDERICK THE GREAT & THE SEVEN YEARS' WAR *by F. W. Longman.*

LEONAUR

ALSO FROM LEONAUR

AVAILABLE IN SOFTCOVER OR HARDCOVER WITH DUST JACKET

THE 9TH—THE KING'S (LIVERPOOL REGIMENT) IN THE GREAT WAR 1914 - 1918 *by Enos H. G. Roberts*—Mersey to mud—war and Liverpool men.

THE GAMBARDIER *by Mark Severn*—The experiences of a battery of Heavy artillery on the Western Front during the First World War.

FROM MESSINES TO THIRD YPRES *by Thomas Floyd*—A personal account of the First World War on the Western front by a 2/5th Lancashire Fusilier.

THE IRISH GUARDS IN THE GREAT WAR - VOLUME 1 *by Rudyard Kipling*—Edited and Compiled from Their Diaries and Papers—The First Battalion.

THE IRISH GUARDS IN THE GREAT WAR - VOLUME 1 *by Rudyard Kipling*—Edited and Compiled from Their Diaries and Papers—The Second Battalion.

ARMOURED CARS IN EDEN *by K. Roosevelt*—An American President's son serving in Rolls Royce armoured cars with the British in Mesopatamia & with the American Artillery in France during the First World War.

CHASSEUR OF 1914 *by Marcel Dupont*—Experiences of the twilight of the French Light Cavalry by a young officer during the early battles of the great war in Europe.

TROOP HORSE & TRENCH *by R.A. Lloyd*—The experiences of a British Lifeguardsman of the household cavalry fighting on the western front during the First World War 1914-18.

THE EAST AFRICAN MOUNTED RIFLES *by C.J. Wilson*—Experiences of the campaign in the East African bush during the First World War.

THE LONG PATROL *by George Berrie*—A Novel of Light Horsemen from Gallipoli to the Palestine campaign of the First World War.

THE FIGHTING CAMELIERS *by Frank Reid*—The exploits of the Imperial Camel Corps in the desert and Palestine campaigns of the First World War.

STEEL CHARIOTS IN THE DESERT *by S. C. Rolls*—The first world war experiences of a Rolls Royce armoured car driver with the Duke of Westminster in Libya and in Arabia with T.E. Lawrence.

WITH THE IMPERIAL CAMEL CORPS IN THE GREAT WAR *by Geoffrey Inchbald*—The story of a serving officer with the British 2nd battalion against the Senussi and during the Palestine campaign.

Printed in January 2023
by Rotomail Italia S.p.A., Vignate (MI) - Italy